A Path to Academic Leadership

8 Lessons to Advance Your University Career

By Heiko Spallek

Cover image © Sophia Spallek

www.innovativeinkpublishing.com
Send all inquiries to:
4050 Westmark Drive
Dubuque, IA 52004-1840

Contents

Contact

Heiko Spallek
Website: https://linktr.ee/heikospallek
E-mail: heiko@spallek.com
Book website: https://www.spallek.com/leadership

Foreword by Dr. Karl Haden

If you are an aspiring or current leader in search of a concise and actionable guide on academic leadership—an atlas to which you can return repeatedly for direction—Dr. Heiko Spallek has authored this book for you. The post-COVID-19 world presents academic leaders with a confluence of challenges and opportunities: demographic shifts, rising costs, and waning public confidence in higher education demand innovative leadership. Technological innovations propelled by the pandemic, such as online and hybrid learning models, unlock new possibilities alongside the emerging potential of artificial intelligence (AI). This book will equip you with the tools and strategies to achieve outstanding results while navigating fresh challenges and capitalizing on emerging opportunities.

By the author's own admission, *A Path to Academic Leadership, 8 Lessons to Advance Your University Career* is an exploration based on his personal life-long journey. While I've worked with thousands of higher education leaders during my career, a few individuals stand out for their ability to traverse a path to leadership at an accelerated pace. I first met Dr. Spallek 15 years ago as an assistant professor at a leadership institute I led. A highly motivated participant, he set a 10-year goal of becoming an associate dean for curriculum. Even as an assistant professor, Dr. Spallek had already accumulated a lifetime of experiences that gave him remarkable insight on life in general and higher education in particular. Over the decade after our paths first crossed, Dr. Spallek hurdled over his initial goal and traveled across the globe to serve as Head of School and Dean at the University of Sydney School of Dentistry.

Because I've had the privilege to accompany Dr. Spallek on segments of his journey, I recognize in the book some of the landmarks we've seen together. For example, he and I discovered the Harvard Study of Adult Development together (Lesson 1: "Be Nice"). I'm convinced that the reader will benefit from knowing more about how his philosophy influenced his leadership practice. Fifteen years ago, during the leadership institute days, when asked about his core values, Dr. Spallek told me that he was committed to evidence-based action, in education, leadership and management, and across all facets of life. He also shared his belief that the only way one can advance in life and in one's profession is to read and study widely, not just in one's field or specialty. Aristotle, someone who has influenced my view of leadership, would say that Dr. Spallek exhibits *practical wisdom*, the virtue that enables a person to apply knowledge and reason effectively in real-world scenarios through sound decision making and right action. Higher education, indeed, the world, needs more leaders with practical wisdom.

From running committees to communicating through storytelling, every page in *A Path to Academic Leadership, 8 Lessons to Advance Your University Career* includes tested, evidence-based guidance to succeed as an academic leader. While Dr. Spallek acknowledges in Lesson 7: "Be Smart" that "I do have the problem that I cannot remember everything," the reader may doubt his humble confession. He supports each lesson with an extraordinary synthesis of ideas, examples, and data from books and articles he has consumed on his path to leadership. I encourage readers who want to dig deeper to explore the annotated references. By the time I finished reading the book manuscript, I had ordered three additional texts described in the Further Readings sections.

A Path to Academic Leadership, 8 Lessons to Advance Your University Career is your roadmap to thriving in higher education leadership. Whether you are a faculty member aiming to grow as a leader or a seasoned administrator, Dr. Spallek has written an indispensable resource to equip you with the essential attitudes, behaviors, and skills to navigate the unique challenges of the academic environment.

N. Karl Haden, PhD, is a philosopher, an entrepreneur, and the founder and president of the Academy for Advancing Leadership (AAL), a strategic consulting and talent development firm in Atlanta, Georgia. He is the author of numerous articles and monographs on leadership and educational policy. He is also the coauthor, with Rob Jenkins, of *The 9 Virtues of Exceptional Leaders* (Deeds, 2015) and *31 Days With the Virtues* (Deeds, 2020).

Acknowledgments

Many have traveled with me during my decades-long leadership journey—they have continuously provided feedback, served as role models, or have actively mentored me. Then, there are the ones who have formed my understanding of leadership through books, articles, and podcasts—most of them don't even know I have benefited from. Notably, Elsbeth Kalenderian and Joseph Kerr have provided invaluable feedback to the manuscript and prevented me from saying things the wrong way. And of course, I am grateful to Jen Wreisner who made my language clearer weeding out my "German accent." I have attempted to provide links and references to the most influential authors throughout the book. Here is my feeble attempt to list a few of the most influential people—a list that has naturally many omissions:

Vale Frazer Allan, PhD
Tanja Bekhuis, PhD, MS, MLIS
Simon Bronitt, LLB, LLM
James Deschner, DMD, PhD
Chuck Friedman, PhD
Karl Haden, PhD
John Halamka, MD, MS
Zsuzsa Horvath, PhD
Sara Hurley, BDS, MSc, MA
Lynn Johnson, PhD
Elsbeth Kalenderian, PhD, DMD
Tom Kennie, MBA, PhD

Joseph Kerr, MBA, PMP
Kathleen Matthews, BDS
Andrew McLachlan AM, PhD, FPS, FACP, MCPA, MSHPA
Bill O'Reilly, AM, BDS
Alan Pettigrew, BSc, PhD, DSc (h.c.)
Jennifer Potts, BSc, PhD
Kathryn Refshauge, OAM, PhD
Janice Clare Reid, AC, FASSA, FRSN
Brad Rindal, DDS
Lesley Russell Wolpe, PhD
Titus Schleyer, DMD, PhD
Gisela Spallek, MD, Dr. Med., MSBA
Rick Valachovic, DMD, MPH
Muhammad Walji, MS, PhD
Robyn Ward, AM, MBBS, PhD, FRACP, FAHMS, FQA
Stephen Weller, PhD
Robert Weyant, MS, DMD, DrPH
And many more …

Introduction

…There are plenty of leadership books that explain the theory behind good leadership much better than this one—mainly because smarter authors wrote them. To name just two, John Kotter in his *Leading Change* explains the different frames of leadership (Kotter, 2012), and Karl Haden in his *The 9 Virtues of Exceptional Leaders: Unlocking Your Leadership Potential* shares the virtues of excellent leadership (Haden, 2015). Don't get me wrong: as an academic, I love these theoretical frameworks, but how much do they help us on a practical day-to-day level?

This book explores a lifelong journey of evolving leadership knowledge, skills, and philosophy, giving life to these concepts through real-world context. Spanning over three continents and numerous leadership roles, beginning with forced service in the East German military and arriving in the present day as Head of School and Dean of The University of Sydney School of Dentistry, my road was filled with formal and informal learning, life experience, and opportunities to learn from the very best, the not so good, and much in between. How was the road paved? Active effort and learning went into seeking good mentors, learning from existing leadership and management resources, observation of others, and many personal failures and successes. Although this book expresses subjective viewpoints, it draws on much evidence from the leadership literature without the so often associated hype that such resources come with. Intertwined in this personal story are pointers to more reading, in most instances, both long and short resources. Through the magnifying lens of time, the following pages present the views of only one academic. Understandably there may be a concern that leadership "rules" derived from one leader based on recall may be biased either by socially desirable responses to reflect expected behavior or the vagaries of memory over long periods. Hopefully, you will find at least some relief from this concern in knowing much of this writing is supported by my journal (Commonplace Book; Pipes, 2016) that has been in place for more than a decade and feedback from hundreds of readers of my weekly *Leadership Travel Guide Newsletter* (Spallek, 2024).

What to Expect?

Hopefully, the book strikes the right balance of helping aspiring academic leaders with valuable content without overwhelming them—this book can be read in half a day. While not wanting to offend anyone, it appears strange when authors publish 300+ page tomes on leadership, but they have never run more than a consultancy with three subcontractors. On the other hand, reading about the leadership style of industry tycoons such as Steve Jobs, Elon Musk, or Jack Welch is enjoyable, but how practical are their experiences when you lead a team of 25 researchers inside a large multilayered university?

You will notice the extensive use of quotes and references, reflecting the belief that there is no good reason for reinventing the wheel. We live in a world of information overflow but are short on attention. While reading a lot on leadership, I find that many books and business school articles sell snake oil as they are often written by people who do not lead organizations and therefore have time to write books. That is not entirely fair, but you see where I am heading …. Occasionally, I find something valuable and apply it in practice—only then I included the resource in this book, sparing you the time-consuming culling process. Thus, read this book as you would read a "guidebook," allowing you, the reader, to explore what was seen along the path for more than three decades. Learn from the journey; at minimum, you can learn from my mistakes.

The goal is not to add just another book on your shelf that looks good in a Zoom meeting background but to bring together a collection of resources and experiences that are relevant and helpful for a career in a university. When you read a section that you find "just interesting," go on and continue reading; but when a theme resonates with you and you would like to dig deeper, the provided resources will allow you to explore the topic in depth. I am curious to hear readers' judgment on my selection.

And most importantly, this guide helps you adjust and chart your leadership journey. My friend Joe Kerr shared with me one of his favorite 1968 quotes from Thomas Merton when he read the draft manuscript: "People may spend their whole lives climbing the ladder of success only to find, once they reach the top, that the ladder is leaning against the wrong wall." How fitting!

Like every decent book these days, *A Path to Academic Leadership* comes with an online resource. The publisher says this improves sales, but the real purpose is to offer a dynamic compilation of resources with links, so you do not have to manually type any of the links found in the reference list at the end of this book. The leadership journey continues; undoubtedly, some readers will reach out with welcome new suggestions and ideas. These will be collected and added to the website. Please use the compilation to get inspirations and ideas: http://www.spallek.com/leadership/.

What is the minimum number of people you need to have working for you to benefit from this book? The answer is evident in my mind: One! And this one person can be yourself. Don't you lead yourself, set goals in life, look for advancement opportunities, and interact with others? You could be a mother "leading" two teenagers toward a successful career or a casual academic in a research lab "leading" yourself to more research funding and fulfilling roles. While I often use the term "staff" when talking about people you lead, in almost all instances, "staff" can be replaced with "undergraduate students," "PhD students," "committee members," or "a loud crowd of students" (whether they cheer you up or chant slander because you represent an unpopular university decision—happened to me a week before writing these lines). The actual test and need for leadership excellence often come in settings where you do not have any formal authority over the individuals you want to influence and encourage to move in a particular direction.

Warning! This is not your book if you want to impress others with business school jargon. If you are starting a PhD in organizational psychology or management of change, this is not your book. If you speak at academic leadership conferences and are searching for conference keynote pabulum, you should find another book or search on YouTube. Some early readers of drafts, mainly the ones from the academe, have suggested that I should make the book longer, adding more theory and a science-based framework. I disagree. Authentic leaders are busy people; they want guidance and want to save time. Also, there are enough academic leadership books around to satisfy any theorist.

My career path: As the son of an upholsterer and a seamstress, I grew up in East Berlin, where I studied dentistry at the Berlin Charité. But before studying dentistry, I had to serve in the East German military. Being raised by my parents to be very critical of the Communist regime, I did not want to guard the Wall and potentially be forced to shoot at people who attempted to flee the country. Thus, I signed up for four years as an officer, allowing me to select my three-year deployment based on availability. So, in the first training year, I learned how to build military-style bridges to blow them up afterward with a lot of TNT. Then, I was deployed in the Special Construction Support Battalion in Berlin, supporting the redevelopment of the Berlin Charité. I left each morning with 80 recruits to the construction site to help the inefficient East German construction companies by assigning the recruits to menial tasks. When I started the deployment, I was 19 years old, and the youngest of the recruits assigned to me was 22. Many of them were selected for "construction duty" because their criminal history prevented them from being deployed in troops that carried weapons.

At 23, I started studying dentistry which initially included four main subjects: anatomy, physiology, biochemistry, and Marxism-Leninism. This, fortunately, changed suddenly during the second year of my studies as the iron curtain fell, opening a new world for my peers and me. I feel lucky to have experienced the collapse of the Communist system and the fall of the Berlin Wall. While most people talk about this figuratively, I could see it quite literally in person as the Berlin wall was right next to the dental school in Berlin, visible from our seminar room windows. That societal change of seeing democracy rise was a formative experience that shaped my understanding of freedom of speech, social justice, authority, and democracy. The experiences allowed me to have different views, and they have shaped my approach to inclusive leadership, especially the appreciation for other viewpoints, which is at the core of effective leadership. The fact that the Communist regime told the people so many "fairy tales" about political and economic progress in a country clearly on the path to failure formed my love for data as a basis for decision-making instead of opinions.

I thrived in the new environment, suddenly not treated as a second-rated person anymore because I had refused to join the Communist party and finished dental school as valedictorian of my 1993 graduating class. I got a Dr. med. dent. in dental material sciences from the Humboldt University in Berlin. I then worked as an Assistant Professor in the Periodontics Department at the Charité dental clinic. In 1996, I moved to the United States, where I worked in the first department of dental informatics in Philadelphia. Because I did not just want to rely on informal learning, I got a Computer and Information Sciences degree from Temple University's Fox School of Business. At that time, I had the choice between an academic position that would keep me connected with periodontology or a research position that could provide an opportunity to affect oral health outcomes in a broader sense. There are many good people in periodontology, so I am not sure I could have added much to their work.

In parallel, my wife and I built a technology consulting company to serve health-care professionals. The business thrived under my wife's leadership for over 20 years until we sold the company to our Chief Technology Officer. During my career, I have developed a reckless disregard for the boundaries of disciplines. In 2002, I moved to the University of Pittsburgh, a more research-oriented institution, ranked fifth in the United States in annual research funding. My academic activities consisted initially of 80% research, 10% teaching and 10% service. This balance shifted in 2010 upon becoming Associate Dean for Faculty Development and Information Management to about 80% administration and 20% research. I was responsible for the dental school's annual staff reviews, academic career progression, promotions, recruitment, and retirement. While in Pittsburgh, I served on boards of start-up companies and attempted to commercialize various software ventures. Regretfully, none of them was purchased by Google or their peers. However, they provided ample learning opportunities but limited financial gain.

Then in 2016, seeking new opportunities, challenges, and different perspectives, the journey took another turn to Professor and Deputy Dean of the then Faculty of Dentistry at the University of Sydney, Australia. In 2018, a new leadership adventure began, first appointed as Acting Dean and then as Head of School and Dean of the now Sydney Dental School.

In 2019, I was appointed as Academic Lead for Digital Health and Health Service Informatics for the Faculty of Medicine and Health at the University of Sydney, in addition to my leadership role in dentistry. Then, in 2021, I was elected chair of the University's Heads of School committee, which includes 35+ school leaders across all academic fields at the University of Sydney. I currently serve on the Scientific Advisory Committee of one dental technology company in Australia (Dentroid, based in Canberra) and volunteer as a board member of a not-for-profit organization that provides tailored services to people with disabilities (Community Connections Australia, based in Parramatta).

Be Nice

"If you are humble and grateful, your people will be humble and grateful."
Michael Hyatt, founder and CEO of Michael Hyatt & Company.

I want to start with a fundamental behavior: Be nice! When I give leadership talks, I have often received a peculiar dichotomy of feedback related to this Lesson. There are voices from people who belong to middle management or below who are incredibly grateful that I have mentioned polite behavior as an essential leadership quality. But I have received equally often utter astonishment from members of the executive management or senior academic leaders, who find it insulting that I suggest that not all leaders behave politely all the time. They claim that being polite is so apparent that it should not be mentioned. I will leave it to you to draw conclusions from these opposing viewpoints.

Everyone is busy and stressed during these challenging times! However, this is no excuse for being impolite. If you are rude to your staff, they will see this as an invitation to be disrespectful to their staff, clients, customers, or students. If you are late to meetings, your people will be late to meetings. If you are angry and defensive when you get negative feedback, your people will be angry and defensive when they get negative feedback. This, of course, also applies to the passive-aggressive behavior that we see in some people. Leaders' behaviors matter, and public discourse influences people's behavior in the workplace. Michael Hyatt points out that your people will mimic you: "If you are humble and grateful, your people will be humble and grateful. If you are warm and engaging, your people will be warm and engaging" (Hyatt, 2009). Therefore, we, as leaders, must set a positive example. We can only push culture in the right direction if we acknowledge and reward appropriate behavior. If someone is warm and engaging, for instance, by comforting a staff member in distress or by helping a student in need, such as setting up a food pantry during the COVID-19 crisis, we as leaders must acknowledge such acts of kindness and positively reinforce that behavior.

Leadership researcher and book author Christine Porath calls nice behavior "civility" and notes that it "elicits perceptions of warmth and competence" and lifts people up, paying dividends for an organization. On the flip side, she writes, supported by scientific studies, that "incivility shuts people down in other ways, too. Employees contribute less and lose their conviction" (Porath, 2015). In her TED talk, she argues that respecting your coworkers will advance your career. In her science-backed talk, "she shares surprising insights about the costs of rudeness and shows how little acts of respect can boost your professional success—and your company's bottom line" (Porath, 2018).

Being nice to people you agree with is easy, but what about people who are against you personally or against the values that you stand for? A certain amount of opposition is simply an unpleasant but unavoidable part of being a leader, writes Rob Jenkins (Jenkins, 2020). "It usually means you're doing something right." Most leaders want to be nice and please their team members, but this is not always possible when you must make hard decisions about redundancies in times of financial difficulties or when selecting someone for a position over others. When you make these decisions, you will affect people's lives and must communicate your decisions in a kind, respectful and polite way. This might be hard when you interact with people who strongly oppose your decisions and might have sometimes used abusive or threatening language against you personally or inspired others to scheme against you. However, you should consider that people will forget what you tell them, but they will never forget how you made them feel.

We as leaders need to be open to critique ourselves. We should actively welcome different opinions and encourage our staff to have a voice and speak up when we make mistakes or say something that makes them feel uncomfortable. Again, none of us, I hope, will intentionally make someone else feel miserable, but we sometimes do not know what triggers other peoples' feelings and what makes them anxious. An environment in which every team member can be criticized, except the boss, will hardly foster an open discussion when something goes wrong in a conversation. We need to acknowledge our own weaknesses and mistakes!

How can you make your staff (and family) happy? The Harvard Study of Adult Development (Harvard Medical School, 2015) shows that happy relationships at home and work are essential for all of us. The study followed the lives of 268 Harvard sophomores in 1938 over the last eight decades and found, according to the current director of the study Robert Waldinger, a psychiatrist at Massachusetts General Hospital and a professor of psychiatry at Harvard Medical School, "that our relationships and how happy we are in our relationships has a powerful influence on our health. Taking care of your body is important, but tending to your relationships is a form of self-care too" (Mineo, 2017). In his TED talk, Waldinger states about happiness that it isn't "about wealth or fame or working harder and harder. The clearest message that we get from this 75-year study is this: Good relationships keep us happier and healthier. Period. We have learned three big lessons about relationships. The first is that social connections are really good for us and that loneliness kills. It turns out that people who are more socially connected to family, to friends, to community, are happier, they are physically healthier, and they live longer than people who are less well connected. And the experience of loneliness turns out to be toxic. People who are more isolated than they want to be from others find that they are less happy, their health declines earlier in midlife, their brain functioning declines sooner and they live shorter lives than people who are not lonely. And the sad fact is that at any given time, more than one in five Americans will report that they're lonely" (Waldinger, 2015).

How Can We Address Incivility?

On a formal level, we can remind our staff to follow the institution's Code of Conduct. While this is usually a lengthy and very formal document, it provides the guiding principle for each institution. I frequently remind people of the Code and ask them to reread it, as most have long forgotten it from their orientation.

As many have defined it, culture is the behavior that we individually and collectively tolerate. Thus, we must call out inappropriate behavior. But before addressing this, let us turn to an example of the stress and impact bad behavior can cause. After calling out bad behavior by a senior academic during a school staff training session about culture, a female academic told me:

> *I think that (calling out the senior academic) just happened in the heat of the moment because it made me so mad—to hear the way that two*

men got increasingly loose with their private 'public' conversation, lamenting the loss of a communal lunchroom where you could bump into each other to gripe about work colleagues, and say things like…. I immediately felt disappointed that it seemed as though no-one noticed. I remember thinking—Am I over-reacting? How can I handle this? Should I have a private conversation with him later? I didn't think raising a complaint about it could achieve anything. So I just pointed out that it wasn't appropriate to talk in that way at work. I still think about this incident from time to time, and can clearly remember the room, where we were sitting, etc. These things do have an impact on the subjects of it (bad behavior). I think one of the reasons that bad behavior isn't called out publicly much is that situations like that are so evocative, and can happen quickly to be able to think clearly about questions such as, what can I say? What language should I use? How could I express that what happened then was not ok? Choosing what to battle is another consideration. How much conviction do you hold about something to pursue it, or to decide to let it ride?

How do we create a culture that permits staff to offer feedback without agonizing about the decision to speak up and without fearing the escalation of going "into battle," maybe even resulting in an HR complaint? Applying some fundamental principles of assessment and feedback can be helpful here. In academia, we spend much effort assessing students against standards, yet we often need to apply the same to our staff. We encourage staff to develop skills in having difficult conversations with students, but the same should apply to staff. It works when I express my feelings instead of phrasing the problem as an accusation. The moment we accuse someone of having made, for instance, a racist remark, the only response option for the accused person is denial and rejection, assuming here that none of our staff would declare themselves a racist. We must acknowledge that making a remark interpreted as racist by one or even many other people might not have been made intentionally. This doesn't make the comment acceptable, but it should modulate our response. Assuming that one can determine another person's intentions is quite challenging, as many of us need more awareness of our own intentions. The only thing we can, for sure, and should do, is reflect on our own feelings. Expressing how a statement by someone else has made us feel or impacted us will not automatically trigger a denial response. It is hard to argue with someone who states that something made them sad or anxious. It gives an opening for a discussion instead of the immediate "fight" response. I have personally experienced people reacting quite well to the approach "when you said …, I felt like …" instead of the more aggressive "you did this terrible thing" way of phrasing a critique.

The biggest enemy of polite behavior is the overuse of e-mail as a communication channel—thus, there is a whole section about e-mail in the Lesson 7: "Be Smart." E-mail seems to have multiplied the rudeness of civil correspondence. In public institutions, most e-mail is considered public record and can be subpoenaed. Regardless of public record laws, e-mail is easily shared, and respect for privacy is limited, so if you do not want to read it on the internet or testify to it in court, e-mail is not the solution. E-mail is also tone-deaf. It is easy for people to read it with an entirely different emotional perception than you intended. Almost no week goes by, during which I remind one of my staff that e-mail is not an instrument to resolve conflict. I stress that e-mail is a very efficient communication tool—I use it frequently as a quick count of my Sent Items folder will reveal (~4,000 e-mails per month). However, the moment you notice even the slightest misunderstanding in an e-mail conversation or detect a small appearance of conflict, stop using e-mail and walk over to your communication partner or pick up the phone if this is impossible. Hint for Millennials: *Picking up the phone* is an old saying which means you use the voice function of your phone, bypassing the text message function.

Providing Feedback Is Good ...

Many of you will have read *The Every*, the electrifying follow-up to *Sunday Times* bestseller *The Circle* by Dave Eggers (Eggers, 2021). This novel describes a near-future dystopian world that hopefully will remain in the realm of fiction. In short, the book depicts a time after Apple, Amazon, Facebook, and Google merged and essentially ruled the world. Features common in social media, fitness and dating apps have made it not only into our everyday lives but into our workplaces. The technology described raises many privacy concerns in addition to its potential impact on the users' well-being. In other words, the novel suggests a dark future. One of the book's key themes is that providing feedback to staff is a good thing; if this feedback can be augmented by feedback from coworkers and clients, it is even better. We know that a 360-performance review is a valuable evaluation tool that solicits feedback about an employee from all directions: their managers, coworkers, and direct reports. Novel Human Capital Management (HCM) systems permit all employees to solicit feedback and even get unsolicited feedback from coworkers to augment their performance evaluations. As leaders, we should encourage feedback, but we need to balance between giving feedback and our duty of care about our staff's well-being. In other words, ensure that we are being nice. We must be aware that peer feedback can quickly become a popularity contest if we are not careful. Do we want technology to help us accumulate the increasing feedback we receive about each staff member? For instance, should AI weigh feedback from different sources to create a composite score for each person, which is then used for promotion and career advancement? When the social media revolution started, it was heralded as the ultimate tool for improving access to reliable information through user-generated content and enhancing democracy by allowing everyone to say what they think. Few would support these claims now. Being nice as leaders means keeping our staff safe by carefully vetting any new social-media style feedback gimmicks for the workplace. In Eggers' world, staff members frantically collect feedback from others, mostly about their interactions with others and less about their work. None of them work much, as they are kept busy with scoring interactions and providing feedback. They are stressed to the point of mental breakdown as the company "de-employs" the staff with the bottom 10% of the compounded feedback score. Providing feedback is good, isn't it?

There are other opportunities to get honest feedback about your performance that can be helpful to become a more successful leader. When you move to a new position, you can ask your direct reports to write a short manual on how to best work with you. As you depart, they will be brave enough to be honest and critical. Ask them to write a one-pager about you that answers the following questions: (1) What brings out the best in me, and what brings out the worst in me? (2) What do you wish you would have known about me on day one? (3) Where are my blind spots? Then, make one document out of the submissions and then share this manual with future teams that want to work with you.

New Leader in a Hostile Environment

As academic leaders, we might be confronted with a new leadership role in an organization ripe for change but full of recalcitrant academics. Most new leaders will have a good understanding of what needs to be done; after all, that allowed them to land the job in the first place. However, being nice to your staff when dealing with adversarial attitudes is difficult. When I studied computer science, I learned about the principle of "explore versus exploit." It encapsulates the idea that when you encounter a new environment, exploring makes sense—you listen and investigate what the environment contains. Then, at a certain point, you switch from exploring to exploiting—of course, not in the sense of exploiting the staff who work for you, but in exploiting the policies and processes you find in the organization.

One way to facilitate such an exploration that shifts rapidly and at a defined time point to exploitation is using a formal process, such as Mandersheid's New Manager Assimilation Program (Manderscheid, 2008). The goal is here to allow you in your new leadership position to learn about your staff and build relationships with each staff member, allowing you to transform your staff into a high-performing team.

The actual process is best described by Hastings et al. as "to help new leaders learn, adapt, and build relationships with their new team in an accelerated and facilitated fashion. This intervention is typically facilitated by an external professional leadership development consultant and generally occurs about 60–90 days after the new leader has started working in the organization. During the assimilation process, the facilitator meets with the leader's team and solicits general feedback. The facilitator then arranges the feedback into themes and has a one-on-one coaching session with the leader to share the feedback. After the coaching session, the leader with the help and presence of the facilitator, meets with the team to have an open dialogue regarding the feedback. This leader assimilation process allows early facilitated feedback and open dialogue between the leader and team, which can be important in transitioning the new leader with the organization" (Hastings et al., 2018).

While this method is not the panacea of onboarding for leaders in complex environments, it might help you be perceived as a nice and caring new leader who tries to understand the complexities of the organization you have just joined.

Learn to Be Polite

This subheading sounds like my mother talking, but how can we truly learn to be polite and nice? This is very easy when talking to nice and polite people who agree with us. Everyone can do that! But what about having these difficult conversations that make you anxious in the morning when you see them on your calendar?

The first step to having good conversations with people who disagree with us is to have better conversations with ourselves. Start to focus on becoming more self-aware by observing your own thoughts without judgement. In other words, controlling your emotions gives you more degrees of freedom if you find yourself in a controversial situation. Your staff will pick up on this, consciously or subconsciously, and you will start changing the culture. For instance, when you are angry, how long are you locked up in the prison of this mental state? You actually decide how long you want to stay angry. If you are self-aware, you can get off this path before you say something you yourself regret afterward or something that your HR colleagues will be unhappy about later on.

Generally, we all do too much rumination. You don't have to finish the arguments you had with your staff in your head after the meeting is over. But too often, we repeat the conversation which just happened in our heads. However, the moment we leave the meeting, we are talking to ourselves. We know how the conversation went! Who are we telling this in our heads? Some might argue that if we want to improve our performance when talking to difficult people, we should analyze later what happened and how we could have done it better to learn from it for the next time. I call this a *critical* analysis! Or we should prepare for difficult conversations by playing them out in our heads well before the conversation occurs. I call this *proper preparation*! I am referring here to rumination (a fancy word for thinking about something repeatedly) and, to be precise, the endlessly ongoing kind. Brené Brown writes, "Mindfulness requires that we not be 'over-identified' with thoughts and feelings, so that we are caught up and swept away by negative reactivity." and that we say to ourselves things like, "… you're so stupid!" which most of us would never think of saying to others (Brown, 2018). Eckhart Tolle described it well in Chapter 3 of *The Power of Now*, explaining that learning from the past is good, but endless remorse is not (Tolle, 2010).

I try to bring my attention and energy to the present moment (Tolle, 2010), which is hard given that a recent study published in Science reports that almost half of our thoughts are unrelated to what we are doing (Killingsworth & Gilbert, 2010). You can achieve better focus with Mindfulness or other contemplative techniques to live, what Sam Harris calls, an examined life (Harris, 2014). Others call this emotional intelligence—the practice of recognizing, understanding, and ultimately controlling your own emotions and, by doing so, recognizing, understanding, and empathizing with the emotions of others. Whatever you call it, it is crucial to be effective when interacting with people or working alone. We are prone to distraction; more about this under the Lesson 2: "Cultivate Humility"; the more we overcome this tendency, the more we get done. Edmund Husserls coined the effort to direct your attention as "Blickstrahl der Aufmerksamkeit" (Becker, 2009). This German phrase tries to express attentional agency as a ray of attention or, more literally, a spotlight of attention (Metzinger, 2009). If we effectively control this ray, we can direct our attention to the present moment or initiate a shift of attention to an object of interest, such as the emotional state of our conversation partner, instead of the focus on our own emotions. Another way to explain this critical skill is by noting who cannot sufficiently control attention, such as infants who initially cannot even control their visual attention or adults during the dream state or when afflicted by drunkenness or mental disease. We should live in the moment, for each is an opportunity for a new beginning.

Not only in leadership situations but all the time, it is important to change from feelings of resentment to resilience. I do not refer to resentment directed against others but against ourselves. We all tend to make mistakes because we are humans (I do more than my share!), and then we generally think too much about these past mistakes and criticize ourselves. And then, naturally, we start worrying about the future. But how do we improve? Not by beating ourselves up about past mistakes or worries about the future, but by trying again and again, utilizing learnings from each failed attempt to internalize the knowledge gained. Every athlete or musician will confirm that thinking about mistakes will not improve performance, but training and practice do: we must adopt this in our everyday lives as leaders! In other words: Be more generous to yourself because generosity creates happiness.

Being in the right mindset is essential for success at the very top, not just in academic leadership. What can we learn from top athletes? Most people think that it is crucial for top athletes to be super fit and have top technical skills in their sports, but it takes more to become World Number 1. A podcast with Ben Crowe, Ash Barty's mindset coach, explains how Ben enables top athletes such as Ash, to succeed (Kanowski & Fidler, 2021). Ben uses counter-intuitive approaches, "rather than telling these elite sports people they're the best, Ben encourages them to see themselves as vulnerable and in need of human connection." I don't have a mindset coach, and I also don't play tennis in Wimbledon—or anywhere else, for that matter. But I try to get in the right mindset with daily meditation. Meditation brings me back to full conscious awareness, where I can exercise choice and intention of emotions.

Prepare for Difficult Conversations

How do we best prepare for difficult conversations with alleged bullies, alleged sexual harassers, requestors for unreasonable accommodations, and underperformers? Many of these conversations can be frustrating and tiresome. You can quickly get the impression that everything must be wrong with your organization. The higher you are up in the hierarchy, the worse it gets. President

Obama observed after he left office: "One of the first things I discovered as President of the United States was that no decision that landed on my desk had an easy, tidy answer" (Obama, 2020).

It is hard to be kind and respectful to people with whom you passionately disagree on important matters, such as gender equality, diversity, or anti-racism. There are, however, ways to rewrite the emotional software of your brain. I have already Mindfulness, Vipassana in Pali, which can help you to stay in the present and be calmer. Another tool is loving-kindness meditation, for which the Pali word is *Mettā*. While this method of changing your emotions, and ultimately your behavior, toward adversarial people seems initially contrived, this Buddhist meditation aims to cultivate unconditional kind attitudes toward oneself and others. The focus is on developing kind intentions toward people by repeating phrases, such as "May you be happy" or "May you be free from suffering" toward target people. The target people change gradually from easy to difficult, beginning with loved ones, then neutral ones, and finally adversarial people (Zeng et al., 2015). Sam Harris, neuroscientist, author, and host of the Making Sense Podcast, explains Mettā meditation at 1:14:00 in his conversation with Peter Attia (Attia & Harris, 2018).

While I write about this under the Lesson 2: "Cultivate Humility," we must acknowledge that we should not shy away from conflict to be nice. That would be dishonest. Instead, we should follow sage advice given by Kate Murphy (Murphy, 2020):

- Remain open, even when you disagree with someone. Try to listen without anxiety when you encounter beliefs that are contrary to yours (Chapter 7).
- Listen fully, all the way up until a person stops speaking. Think about how to respond when the other person has finished speaking (Chapter 9).
- Practice conversational sensitivity, which is when you pick up hidden meanings and nuances in tone (Chapter 10).

Given that the COVID-19 pandemic has moved us more to an online environment, we should also rethink the leadership lessons that we all heard at one point: Do not engage in online conflict resolution! While most sage HR advice will steer us toward face-to-face conversations, away from e-mail, phone calls and video conferences, times have changed. Many universities have embraced working from home for academic staff or are somewhere on the continuum from such a radical approach to some form of flexible work arrangement. For leaders, some uncomfortable performance or behavior discussions need to occur on a video conference platform. What should we keep in mind when having challenging discussions online? First, everything said above still applies. Adam Grant describes a debate between people poetically as a dance—an analogy that has stuck with me: "Good debate is not a war. It's not even a tug-of-war, where you can drag your opponent to your side if you pull hard enough on the rope. It's more like a dance that hasn't been choreographed, negotiated with a partner who has a different set of steps in mind. If you try too hard to lead, your partner will resist. If you can adapt your moves to hers and get her to do the same, you're more likely to end up in rhythm" (Grant, 2021). This can be done online, even if we miss out on a lot of the body language we can only perceive in a 3D world.

Grant reflects on situations that turn hostile: "When someone becomes hostile, if you respond by viewing the argument as a war, you can either attack or retreat. If, instead, you treat it as a dance, you have another option—you can sidestep. Having a conversation about the conversation shifts attention away from the substance of the disagreement and toward the process for having a dialogue. The more anger and hostility the other person expresses, the more curiosity and interest you show. When someone is losing control, your tranquility is a sign of strength. It takes the wind out of their emotional sails."

This sounds good, but where can we see an example? I was impressed by Sam Harris' discussion about vaccines with Eric Topol, one of the most cited biomedical researchers globally. Their conversation aimed to convince people who opposed the COVID-19 vaccination to change their minds. It is specifically about how to "convince the other side"—not about just saying what people who got vaccinated believe anyhow (Harris, 2021).

On a more technical note, we should always adequately set up our video conferencing environment, especially for difficult conversations. Nothing must be more distressing for a staff member than having to sit in front of a computer to see nothing but the black silhouette of their boss—too many scary movies have used that cliché. You also want to ensure that your upper body is visible, not just your head, to convey your body language and instill trust and openness.

A last point about "complicated staff," as we leaders too often must confront people with whom we are not only disagreeing but whom we can't help to morally judge. Some of them might have done things that we find abhorrent, which makes us feel superior or triggers the "duty" of being tough on them. The key here is judging and evaluating what was done, the act, not necessarily the person. When dealing with them, it might be a good idea to remember that these people might have had unfortunate lives, or just a terrible day, or simply made bad decisions. Paul Bloom, Professor of Psychology at Yale University (Campuspress, 2020), mentions in a conversation with Sam Harris, "Nobody is a villain in their own heads. Our impulse for public shaming is corrosive and unhealthy" (Harris, 2020a). Adopting this general attitude helped me to have better uncomfortable conversations.

Further Readings

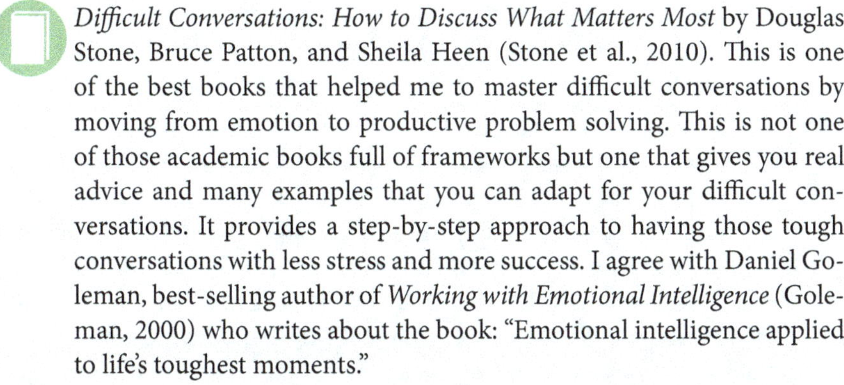

Difficult Conversations: How to Discuss What Matters Most by Douglas Stone, Bruce Patton, and Sheila Heen (Stone et al., 2010). This is one of the best books that helped me to master difficult conversations by moving from emotion to productive problem solving. This is not one of those academic books full of frameworks but one that gives you real advice and many examples that you can adapt for your difficult conversations. It provides a step-by-step approach to having those tough conversations with less stress and more success. I agree with Daniel Goleman, best-selling author of *Working with Emotional Intelligence* (Goleman, 2000) who writes about the book: "Emotional intelligence applied to life's toughest moments."

"7 Tips for Difficult Conversations" by Daisy Dowling, *Harvard Business Review*. If another book is too much for you at this stage, especially as you are reading this one with increasing enthusiasm, here is the abridged version of how to approach difficult conversations (Dowling, 2009).

"14 Ways To Approach Conflict And Difficult Conversations At Work" by the Forbes (Forbes Coaches Council, 2017) offers ideas on approaching dreaded conversations with staff whose conduct or utterances we disagree with.

"Universal Upset Person Protocol Handout" by Dirk Drummond MD (Drummond, 2012b) is a 4-page handout that helps you deal with upset people in all kinds of situations following a 6-step protocol, using interactions with patients as an example. You might also find the accompanying YouTube video (Drummond, 2012a) helpful.

"An Exceptional Leader Presents a Difficult Talk" by Dr Melanie Keep, a successful academic at the Sydney School of Health Sciences at The University of Sydney. I have worked with her on various eHealth projects and value her as a great collaborator and innovator. She shares "Lessons in Leadership" on YouTube (Keep, 2021a)—please note that when you click on the link, the video appears to be an hour long, but her talk starts at 3:23 min and the second half of the video is consumed by Q/A. Her impressive and honest presentation moved and inspired me to rethink my assumptions about leadership, healthcare and changing career goals. All of us should embrace her message about moving from the dancefloor to the balcony (and back) and making space at the table for others to lead. Her powerful piece in the *Medical Journal of Australia* supports her message and reflects on her personal experiences with miscarriage and research gaps (Keep, 2021b).

How to Talk So Kids Will Listen & Listen So Kids Will Talk by Adele Faber and Elaine Mazlish (Faber & Mazlish, 2012). Clearly, you think this is a mistake as a parenting book should not be part of a book on leadership but bear with me and check this out. Faber and Mazlish give advice that will help to deal with many leadership challenges and with your kids.

The Coddling of the American Mind: How Good Intentions and Bad Ideas Are Setting Up a Generation for Failure by Jonathan Haidt and Greg Lukianoff (Haidt & Lukianoff, 2018). This book is not so "American," despite what its title might imply. The lessons can be applied to a global audience—it explores the flip side of inappropriate behavior, the resilience of individuals, or how the authors describe it, antifragility. While it deals mostly with the emotional well-being of college students, many lessons can be applied to your younger staff. The authors observe that younger generations' members increasingly demand protection from words and ideas they do not like. When you read the book, you will notice that this "demand for a safe environment" might prevent our organizations from creating a culture of open conversation that permits low-stake critique and corrective measures. Students or staff should see themselves not as fragile candles but as fires, welcoming the wind by seeking out ideologically different ideas. If individuals are not empowered to "welcome the wind" and speak up about what they feel without anxiety, then people who exhibit inappropriate behavior will dominate the culture.

"The Coddling of the American Mind" by Greg Lukianoff and Jonathan Haidt (Lukianoff & Haidt, 2015). Again, only some people want to read a whole book, so here is a shorter Atlantic article that is a bit narrower in scope and not fully reflective of the book. Their cover story about college students' increasing demand for protection from unwelcome ideas resulted in a long and controversial discussion among the magazine's readers that can be found on the website of *The Atlantic*.

"What Makes Us Happy?" by Joshua Wolf Shenk (Shenk, 2009). If you want to learn more about the connection between happiness and relationships, read about the 268 Harvard men who entered college in the late 1930s and follow some of their stories through war, career, marriage and divorce, parenthood and grandparenthood, and old age in the 2009 Atlantic article by Joshua Wolf Shenk.

"All major decisions about your career will be made when you are not in the room. How do you want people to describe you when you aren't in the room?" Carla Harris, vice chairman of global wealth management, managing director and senior client advisor at Morgan Stanley (Burns, 2014)

Cultivate Humility

"It's amazing what you can accomplish if you do not care who gets the credit."
Harry S. Truman (1884–1972), 33rd president of the
United States from 1945 to 1953.

To be an effective academic leader, you need to exhibit epistemic deference. Or to put it in less lofty terms: most people know more than you do about most subjects, and groups are almost always smarter than the individual. Humility is necessary for learning. It is the virtue that acknowledges one's ignorance while being open to learning. I believe the phrase "I don't know" is a sign of maturity. As a young man, I could not say those words as they were words of shame. Now, I cannot get through the day without a half dozen or so "I don't know" statements.

Sriram Krishnan, a successful product leader across Facebook, Snap, and X (formerly Twitter) who has worked closely with Mark Zuckerberg and Jack Dorsey, reminded us during an interview with Sarthak Haribhakti that leaders often have a huge advantage, "What a lot of people think of as raw IQ from CEOs is actually a) access to information from smart people b) the compounding effects of (a). When you are the founder/CEO of an iconic company, you can tap into the knowledge/expertise/raw intellect of the top percentile in any field of your choosing. The compounding effect of that is remarkable because you can sit at the intersection of many domains and see patterns very few can" (Haribhakti, 2020).

Displaying humility while having access to information from smart people has many different faces and should not be reduced to the occasional self-deprecating statement, but instead should come from a genuine personal recognition that you do not have all the answers. You want to be transparent and share information that is not confidential. We have all observed people who keep information to themselves to have the upper hand in the workplace. They usually stand out, but not for good reasons.

Learn New Things

One way to experience humility is to learn new things. We have, as young adults, often been told to focus our energy on one particular thing and then professionally pursue this area to perfection. Academics in leadership positions have mostly been following this advice, focusing on a narrow field of inquiry, which then permitted them to rise among their peers to a position of leadership through excellence in research and education. As Talbot puts it in a recent *The New Yorker* article (Talbot, 2021), we live in a "competitive, individualistic, allegedly meritocratic society," which means that we cannot do something we are mediocre at if we want to enjoy a healthy career progression. This applies even more so in academia than anywhere else, as we are judged by our societal impact and international achievements. So, should we limit ourselves to be good at one particular thing when we advance our academic careers? Yes absolutely, this is what brought us where we are now. But how do we keep our mental agility? How do we react to an increasingly volatile world? I recently learned that we are not anymore in a VUCA world (Volatile, Uncertain, Chaotic, Ambiguous) but in a GISE world (Global, Interdependent, Scary, Escalating). But regardless of which consulting jargon we use, how do we deal with the business transformations that keep our universities competitive, and how do we react to the constraints that the next pandemic will put on us individually and on our institutions as a whole?

Mental processing speed declines rapidly with age—in some areas already in your late teens. Talbot writes that "Fluid intelligence, which encompasses the capacity to suss out novel challenges and think on one's feet, favors the young. But crystallized intelligence—the ability to draw on one's accumulated store of knowledge, expertise, and Fingerspitzengefühl—is often enriched by advancing age" (I like the German description which means "fingertips feeling"—an intuitive flair or instinct). Keeping our core area of scholarly expertise fresh will ensure that we stay at the top of our game. However, we might benefit from learning new things, which will keep our growth mindset alive and re-calcitrant tendencies away. Talbot cites Stanford psychology professor Carol Dweck, who coined the term "growth mindset, the belief that abilities are not fixed but can improve with effort; a commitment to serious rather than 'hobby learning' (in which 'the learner casually picks up skills for a short period and then quits due to difficulty, disinterest, or other time commitments'); a forgiving environment that promotes what Dweck calls a 'not yet' rather than a 'cannot' approach" (Dweck, 2007). Adam Grant writes in *Think Again: The Power of Knowing What You Don't Know* (Grant, 2021): "When people reflect on what it takes to be mentally fit, the first idea that comes to mind is usually intelligence. The smarter you are, the more complex the problems you can solve—and the faster you can solve them. Intelligence is traditionally viewed as the ability to think and learn. Yet, in a turbulent world, there's another set of cognitive skills that might matter more: the ability to rethink and unlearn. … The curse of knowledge is that it closes your mind to what you don't know. Good judgment depends on having the skill—and the will—to open your mind. A hallmark of wisdom is knowing when it's time to abandon some of the most cherished parts of your identity." This not only applies to your career development but to all aspects of life: I recently learned how to drive a boat in the busy Sydney Harbour and clearly felt like a 16-year-old during my first driving lesson on a highway …

Who Can Teach Us New Things?

Learning new things helps us stay agile and teach us humility by creating a growth mindset crucial for successful academic leadership. The logical question that follows is, "Who can teach us new things?" Academics are often the world's experts in their chosen field of study leaving not many people who can advance their knowledge. Academic leadership roles require domain expertise to ensure proper recognition and standing among peers, but they also require leadership and managerial skills that straddle many areas of expertise. But learning to be a leader goes far beyond learning some accounting and human resource skills! The sociologist Mark Granovetter has advanced the concept of "the strength of weak ties" which posits that our close friends and colleagues know what we know. Only our acquaintances occupy a completely different world and know things we don't. If we want to learn new things, we need to go beyond our staff, close peers and collaborators as the primary sources of new knowledge, ideas and inspiration. Author Malcolm Gladwell (*The Tipping*

Point (Gladwell, 2002) and *Blink* (Gladwell, 2005)) explains this idea in more detail: "Granovetter argues that when it comes to finding out about new jobs—or, for that matter, gaining new information, or looking for new ideas—weak ties tend to be more important than strong ties. Your friends, after all, occupy the same world that you do. They work with you, or live near you, and go to the same churches, schools, or parties. How much, then, do they know that you don't know? Mere acquaintances, on the other hand, are much more likely to know something that you don't. To capture this apparent paradox, Granovetter coined a marvellous phrase: 'the strength of weak ties.' The most important people in your life are, in certain critical realms, the people who aren't closest to you, and the more people you know who aren't close to you the stronger your position becomes" (Gladwell, n.d.).

So, how do we apply this to our academic leadership roles? Make an effort to talk to people beyond your immediate circle of colleagues in your school or faculty and your regular friends. Treat every conversation as a potential learning experience, not as a chore. Create an inclusive and diverse environment of people who challenge you and do not fall into groupthink traps. And ensure cultural safety so they speak up! Don't be afraid to tell other people about yourself or what you do—only then will they be more likely to tell you about themselves. Attend talks, lectures and presentations and read books and articles beyond your immediate interests.

Being Wrong

Too rarely, we reflect on situations that have humbled us. While we do not want to dwell too much on past mistakes (see Lesson 1: "Be Nice"), we need this kind of reflective analysis occasionally to cultivate humility. University of Virginia's McIntire School of Commerce marketing professor David Mick says, "Mahatma Gandhi, an iconic figure renowned for wisdom, was not submissively humble; he was more self-assuredly humble. Reflecting on times you were humbled reminds you not to be submissive, but simply to realize that what we do not know dwarfs what we know. Forgetting that, can encourage overconfidence and cloud one's decision-making ability" (Mick, 2017). Therefore, admitting blunders is an essential facet of showing humility. Increasingly, universities favor committee decisions over executive decision-making by deans and other academic leaders. This makes it much easier for leaders to hide behind these committee decisions when things go wrong or fall into the ISLAGIAT category (a helpful acronym that stands for: It Seemed Like A Good

Idea At The Time). However, standing up for your previous opinions, committee votes, and decisions will earn you the trust of your staff. Including others in discussions and decision-making is to make better decisions and foster a team environment. It should not be to evade the responsibilities of leadership.

It is often hard to report inconvenient truths to superiors. In hindsight, we often see a stunning inability to uncover errors, and when finally the truth comes to light, the information flow to the top is often delayed. A 45-year-old *Harvard Business Review* article seems to be still relevant today (Argyris, 1977). Chris Argyris explains that when reports of failure arrive at middle managers, they often find these reports too open and forthright as they criticize other parts of the organization. Such negative reports usually charge directly or indirectly individuals who are peers or superiors of the middle managers. As a result, information is softened and delayed: "Once the middle managers were convinced that the predictions were valid, they began to release some of the bad news, but they did so in measured doses." I have personally noticed, having lived and worked on three continents, that each culture has its euphemisms for failure, ranging from "This might warrant a reassessment." to "Here is an opportunity for improvement." but usually fall short of the truth "This is a disaster that needs to be stopped immediately."

According to Argyris, the problem with these delays is that "Top management, therefore, continued to speak glowingly about the product, partially to ensure that it would get the financial backing it needed from within the company." which (1) makes it even harder to speak up about the looming disaster, and (2) alienates the lower ranks who have recognized the problem for a long time. Some frontline staff might think that the pretended success is aimed at confusing the competition, while more cynical ones assume incompetence at the top as any well-informed leader surely must know by now.

How can we overcome this problem that plagues so many universities these days? Argyris suggests that "When the process enables the organization to carry on its present policies or achieve its objectives, the process may be called single loop learning. Single loop learning can be compared with a thermostat that learns when it is too hot or too cold and then turns the heat on or off. The thermostat is able to perform this task because it can receive information (the temperature of the room) and therefore take corrective action. If the thermostat could question itself about whether it should be set at 68 degrees, it would be capable not only of detecting error but of questioning the underlying policies and goals as well as its own program. That is a second and more comprehensive inquiry; hence, it might be called double loop learning. When the plant managers and marketing people were detecting and attempting to correct errors in order to manufacture Product X, that was single loop learning. When they began to confront the question whether Product X should be manufactured, that was double loop learning, because they were now questioning underlying organization policies and objectives."

How do we achieve this double loop learning? First, as leaders, we need to ensure that staff members who raise concerns feel that their alertness and loyalty are valued. Second, we need to avoid interacting with those who usually keep quiet about a problem and teach them that doing so harms their reputations. While in crisis mode, these things are hard to do, so attempt to resolve issues early.

Building Trust

High-trust relationships are a hallmark of high-performing organizations. While most academic leaders would agree with this statement, there are considerable variations in how to achieve a high-trust environment. Academic scholars are trained to question traditional assumptions and encouraged to distrust common knowledge to discover new insights. Thus, as academic leaders, you are facing academic staff whose trust is hard to gain but easy to lose. Trust is built on honesty, transparency, and of course, the leader's humility. Having the trust of your team is not just a nice thing to have but vital when quick decisions need to be made or discretion is required to move ahead without consultation in times of crisis. According to Paul J. Zak, director of the Centre for Neuroeconomic Studies, people at high-trust companies, when compared to people at low-trust companies, report 74% less stress, 106% more energy at work, 50% higher productivity, 13% fewer sick days, 76% more engagement, 29% more satisfaction with their lives and 40% less burnout (Zak, 2017). I do not think more reasons are required to motivate us to improve trust! But Zak and his team also found that "having a sense of higher purpose stimulates Oxytocin production, as does trust. Trust and purpose then mutually reinforce each other, providing a mechanism for extended Oxytocin release, which produces happiness." David Klaasen (Klaasen, 2017) has extracted eight leadership behaviors that improve trust:

1. Recognize excellence,
2. Induce "challenge stress,"
3. Give people discretion in how they do their work,

4. Enable job crafting,
5. Share information broadly,
6. Intentionally build relationships,
7. Facilitate whole-person growth, and
8. Show vulnerability.

The last one, "Show vulnerability" relates to this Lesson 2: "Cultivate Humility." I find that showing vulnerability combined with transparency is the most effective tool for increasing the trust of the staff in their leaders. Sarah Jones Simmer, CEO of Found, said in an interview with Shane Parrish that to develop trust, "I think that's where some periodic in-person engagement is necessary. I do also think that is where, as a leader, demonstrating vulnerability and authenticity and sharing something about who you are outside of your work life or something that matters to you, or like sometimes I'll share an embarrassing story or something that I feel like I learned the hard way as a way to engender that vulnerability kind of. Like I'm going to share something with you that feels awkward to me, and I hope that permits you to know that I'm a real human, we're all figuring this out as we go and that you can be equally vulnerable to me because I do think vulnerability helps engender trust. And I think we just have to find ways of engineering that, as I said, in the absence of the stuff that would happen so organically if you were in the same place" (Parrish, 2022b). If we follow this advice as leaders, we can promote a culture where trust is the default approach to all interactions among all staff members. Shane Parrish concludes that "A low trust approach might put a floor on how often you get taken advantage of, but it puts a ceiling on what's possible" (Parrish, 2022a).

Trust via Zoom

Despite increases in video conferencing fidelity, zoom and other platforms still represent a different mode of interaction that will always lack social presence, even if we will eventually go to VR using live-like avatars in 3D. We should start thinking of videoconferencing as a distinct mode, not a currently inferior one that we can eventually upgrade to full social presence by employing better connectivity, investing in better lights or using high-status-suggesting backgrounds.

Sarah Jones Simmer shares during the same interview insights on how to use different channels for different types of interactions. "I think being clear about what happens on what channel. So Slack is our primary form of communication. We try to reserve e-mail for things that require a lot of context or involve external parties. But it shouldn't be like the ongoing day-to-day engine, that Slack is the water cooler in our case. Both the water cooler and I think they're like general workflow management. Text for urgent stuff, phone calls, more than you think. I feel like we've gotten away from picking up the phone and talking to someone. And I don't know about you, but I've been in so many situations where you're like, you know what? The shortcut to this is, I'm just going to call them. Something is being lost in translation. And I think that comes back to the trust piece. Again, voice on voice does build trust more than Slack to Slack does. So trying to be intentional about that."

When we reflect on how our use of e-mail has evolved (and maybe has not evolved for certain people who we all know too well…), it took us a long time to figure out how to use e-mail differently from how we used paper memos which the department's secretary typed. The pandemic has forced us to adopt videoconferencing rapidly. Now, we all need to go back and develop effective ways to use this novel interaction style. Using it to build trust among our staff will take some experimentation.

Trust and Truth

The recent pandemic gave plenty of opportunities to observe which politicians had the trust of the people and could make effective decisions and which ones could not. Given my German heritage, I might point to Chancellor Angela Merkel who "embodies … a cool, measured and rational approach that inspires confidence. High among her leadership qualities is a projection of competence, no doubt enhanced by Germany's success responding to the pandemic" (Ruscio, 2020). Time will tell how this statement will age. What can we learn from her and from the counter examples of Boris Johnson in Great Britain, Jair Bolsonaro in Brazil and Donald Trump in the United States? Ruscio writes in The Conversation "Telling the truth also earns trust. But honesty is more than just conveying basic facts. It is the capacity to explain the crisis, the sacrifice required and the path to a solution. Roosevelt during the Depression, Churchill during World War II, Kennedy during the Cuban Missile Crisis and Bush in the aftermath of 9/11 (at least the immediate aftermath) were granted considerable discretion because they accurately described and credibly interpreted the challenges people faced. During the COVID-19 crisis, medical professionals have told the inconvenient truths about the pandemic. Some political leaders at the national level have offered false hopes and misleading information. That is why trust in medical professionals in the United States far exceeds trust in elected officials. Finally, trust is given when leaders act in the public interest, not their own self-interest." If you as a leader want to have discretion granted and "the room … to maneuver" you need the trust of your team; that trust "depends on … competency, honesty and commitment to the public interest" (Ruscio, 2020).

Power Display

What is the opposite of humility, and how do we display it? Power, described as the ultimate aphrodisiac by Henry Kissinger, shows in the language that you are using. Jones described this humorously in his compilation of quotes by former Secretary of State Henry Kissinger (Jones, 1973). Kissinger even commented on universities: "The reason that university politics is so vicious is because stakes are so small." Power is dangerous as it causes brain damage, as shown by Sukhvinder Obhi, a neuroscientist at McMaster University in Ontario, who "put the heads of the powerful and the not-so-powerful under a transcranial-magnetic-stimulation machine," and "found that power, in fact, impairs a specific neural process, 'mirroring,' that may be a cornerstone of empathy" (Useem, 2017).

What happens when we, as leaders, do not display humility? As a result, organizations can easily fall prey to the HiPPO syndrome. HiPPO stands for the Highest Paid Person in the Office or the Highest Paid Person's Opinion. The acronym describes the tendency for lower-paid staff to defer to higher-paid ones when a decision must be made. While you, as the leader, are supposed to make the final decision on many crucial issues, you do not have to rush in most instances. I quote here again Angela Merkel who said, "I am regarded as a permanent delayer sometimes, but I think it is essential and imperative to take people along and really listen to them in political talks" (Packer, 2014). I have seen decisions made by high-level academic leaders that were patently wrong, and I know from a personal conversation that the people around the leader knew that but were concerned about voicing their dissent. If a narcissistic leader instills so much fear among his (pronoun selected on purpose here!) followers, it might be time to look for a new employment opportunity elsewhere if you do not have the prospect of a change in leadership in the near-term future. Abraham Lincoln famously included some of his greatest critics in his cabinet while retaining the final decision after discussion. He famously said that "everyone gets a vote, and my one counts."

Part of humility is also to recognize that we still discriminate based on gender regarding leadership roles in academia and elsewhere. When Kamala Harris became vice president-elect of the United States it "provoked familiar criticism, based in part on her identity as a woman. Critics find her too angry, too confident, too competitive. But when women do act less competitively, they are seen as less capable of leadership. This is the 'double-bind' women face when aspiring to leadership positions. To overcome it, we need to understand where it comes from. Why do gender norms privilege men as leaders?" (von Rueden, 2020). Learning about behavior and gender norms serves as the first step to reducing gender inequality in leadership in the real world. We need to dismantle patriarchy!

Learn How to Listen

One way to show humility is to be a good listener. We all heard about the importance of active listening, and unfortunately, we are also noticing immediately when someone else just heard about it. Active listening has been described as a social nuisance, particularly when encounters go like this:

Susan: "How are you, Peter?"

Peter: "Susan, I hear you are interested in my personal well-being."

Philosopher Paul Grice's four conversational maxims should guide how we interact with others during conversations and display our respect (Grice, 1975).

- Quality: Your conversation partners expect to hear the truth from you.
- Quantity: You must convey information that they do not already know.
- Relation: Listeners expect in your utterances relevance that logically flows.
- Manner: You want to be reasonably brief, orderly, and unambiguous.

While the above maxims seem obvious and achievable, when encountering the practicality of today's busy lives, they are not easy to live up to. On top, you will have listeners addicted to distractions and start checking their mobile phones.

When was the last time you listened to someone, or someone really listened to you? Kate Murphy writes, "Listening is about curiosity and patience—asking the right questions in the right way. It has the potential to transform our relationships, improve our self-knowledge, and increase our creativity and happiness" (Murphy, 2020). You should ask questions to elicit more information and avoid saying things like, "The same thing happened to me!" thereby putting the focus on yourself. Have genuine interest in wanting to hear and learn more about your conversation partner; they know if you are faking it. Let the other person fully say what he needs to say and not finish their sentences or thoughts. Henry David Thoreau writes, "The greatest compliment that was ever paid me was when one asked me what I thought and attended to my answer" (Thoreau, 1854). I try to put my phone away, not even having it on the table, which is sometimes impossible when I am expecting an "important" call—in these instances I profusely apologize in advance and set the stage that the conversation might, regrettably, be interrupted. I have found that most people accept this and respond more favorably than an ad hoc interruption. Another trick is mentally giving yourself the task of summarizing what the person says, even if you do not plan to provide a summary to your conversation partner or yourself. Doing this will focus your mind on what is important during the conversation, which is only one thing, paying attention. If you stumble and find yourself not being able to do this for parts of what you hear, then this is a good indication that raising a clarifying question might be helpful. Shane Parrish writes when describing the "resonance," the mammalian ability to share deep emotional states, "The nature of these questions in themselves will show to the other person that they are heard, and effort is being made to take them seriously. Just as it is not enough to know, when it comes to human relationships, it is not enough to understand. What is crucial is to show you understand. If empathy is recognizing another's perspective, consideration for the other needs to be externalized from you for it to exist and build rapport. Summarizing and asking questions is a way of feeding back your resonance. Cutting short the conversation, stating opinions, value judgements, your own solutions, or even a lazy 'I see' or 'interesting' does not demonstrate resonance. In fact, you can use 'I understand' as a red flag for someone who does not understand. Often, this is followed by an action that shows a thorough lack of comprehension" (Parrish, 2020b).

Practice Humility

When you take time to connect with your staff beyond the necessary business interactions, you show them respect and demonstrate humility. Most leaders in universities work very hard and long hours, so it is understandable when they do not want to sit down with their staff to have a conversation just for the sake of deepening relationships. Serendipitously occurring meetings or hallway discussions without specific agenda and goals seem like a waste of time, but I have found they pay big dividends over time.

Contrary to popular business wisdom, I do not believe there has to be a rigid line between our private and public lives. Old-school views consider expressing emotions and compassion as vulnerability; today's generation sees such attributes as the glue that binds us. I try to make relationships to staff and students stronger by sharing personal stories and experiences: simple things make a difference, such as when meeting with students letting them know one of my daughters finished the Bachelor of Commerce program and the other one is in the Bachelor of Psychology program at the University where I work, so I have more insight into student life than students might expect from a dean.

I make time for lunches or coffee breaks with early- and mid-career academics. I try to hang out with young academics and students, which is the best medicine against aging. Often, I use walks to talk to people who also travel between different campus locations. Or I make phone calls if I travel alone. Minimizing lost time is important to me as there are only 168 hours in a week, and I desire to use them wisely. Time spent commuting in a car is not very efficient, for instance. Since 2016, I have never used my car in Sydney for work, but instead enjoy the public transport system, which allows me to read, communicate or just engage in deep thinking.

Encourage Dissent

Humility should permit dissent, but we often fail to encourage our staff to speak up—recall the HiPPO syndrome mentioned above. For a long time, I have been searching for a way to legitimizing critique and encourage staff to challenge strategy by identifying potential failure points in the implementation. Then, I read Daniel Kahneman, who introduces the Premortem in his book *Thinking, Fast and Slow* (Kahneman, 2013). Since then, I have used this method often, for instance, when discussing with technology leaders what could go wrong during a software implementation to prevent overconfident optimism. At a crucial juncture in the development of the software system, I gathered the technologists who are naturally convinced of the superiority of the developed software and predict a smooth implementation. I told them, following Kahneman's script, that they shall imagine that a year from now, we are all sitting around the table because of a disastrous outcome of the implementation of the new system. Before updating our LinkedIn profiles to help us find new employment, we will now spend 10 minutes writing down the history of this disaster and the main reasons that led to it. After the time had elapsed, I asked each person to present their disaster history to the group. As the facilitator, I noted failure points and barriers to success on a whiteboard. We then progressed rating the likelihood of each risk concluding with developing mitigation strategies. Kahneman writes, "The premortem has two main advantages: it overcomes the groupthink that affects many teams once a decision appears to have been made, and it unleashes the imagination of knowledgeable individuals in a much-needed direction. As a team converges on a decision—and especially when the leader tips her hand—public doubts about the wisdom of the planned move are gradually suppressed and eventually come to be treated as evidence of flawed loyalty to the team and its leaders. The suppression of doubt contributes to overconfidence in a group where only supporters of the decision have a voice. The main virtue of the premortem is that it legitimizes doubts" (Kahneman, 2013).

Another way to encourage and empower dissenting voices is by actively supporting them. I have learned this from reading the transcript of the June 2021 interview with President Barack Obama on "The Ezra Klein Show," a production of New York Times Opinion (Klein, 2021). Usually, I am suspicious whether leadership lessons learned at that level can be applied to more ordinary academic leadership situations, but I have gathered quite a bit from this thoughtful conversation. Klein reflects on Obama's approach to "mak[e] yourself a person the other person will feel able to listen to, which means sympathizing with their argument, sanding off some of the edges of your own." Obama's response is something academics, not just leaders, can learn from as we too often rely on logic and evidence to strengthen our arguments. Instead, Obama does the opposite "… the best way to win an argument is to first be able to make the other person's argument better than they can. And for me, what that meant was that I had to understand their world view. And I couldn't expect them to understand mine if I wasn't extending myself to understand theirs." I like Obama's honest response to the personal satisfaction one can get out of being "very logical and incisive […] to dismantle their arguments"— something that rings a bell with academics who are used to scholarly debates. However, our goal as leaders is to advance our institution and not necessary win the argument to score points. Trying to improve the other side's arguments might allow us to recognize that our approach is not optimal and that more diverse opinions help us find a better way. Ask yourself, *is it about bringing the organization forward or about showing off that you are smarter?*

Further Readings

"Why we all fall foul of the Dunning-Kruger effect" by Dan John (John, 2020). In this 6-minute video, social psychologist David Dunning explains the Dunning–Kruger effect, named after him and Justin Kruger, stressing the importance of intellectual humility. I find that admitting our shortcomings is especially important in an increasingly polarized world as "it seems as if people are becoming more convinced of their own beliefs and less willing to contemplate other points of view."

You're Not Listening: What You're Missing and Why It Matters by Kate Murphy (Murphy, 2020). Her book starts a bit slow and presents many things I already knew, but you will learn a lot when you keep reading. For instance, I was intrigued by the speech-thought differential, which claims that we can speak about 120–150 words per minute, but can process much more; thus, we are always inclined to think about other things while listening.

If reading a whole book about listening sounds daunting, you could listen to it as an audiobook… Or, you might want to focus on Chapter 12, in which she describes how you can support a conversation instead of shifting it, which I think is probably the most valuable part of Murphy's book (Murphy, 2020).

Think Again: The Power of Knowing What You Don't Know by Adam Grant (Grant, 2021). Grant casts a new light on many leadership virtues that fill the books about management and leadership; for instance, he explains the intricate interplay between humility and confidence and how both can easily become a curse. While his book is not a leadership book, I can quickly see how any leader can benefit from the wisdom he has gained when working with small and large teams as an organizational psychologist who tries to bring social science into the workplace.

Never Eat Alone by Keith Ferrazzi (Ferrazzi & Raz, 2014). This book is a bit cheesy and predominantly geared toward corporate settings, but it clearly brings home many lessons that we all should embrace but usually do not. For instance, I have adopted Ferrazzi's idea of adding a tickler to my calendar, reminding me once a month to get in touch with a person I enjoyed interacting with but with whom I have temporarily lost touch. I also try to make a conscious effort to network with as many people as possible as I believe it is one of the main ingredients of success.

Admin 101 by David D. Perlmutter (Perlmutter, 2019a). I highly recommend this blog post series to anyone pursuing a leadership career in an academic institution.

"How to be a cool headed clinician" by Daniel Sokol (Sokol, 2012). This article sounds very medical, but in my opinion, expressions of empathy need to be displayed by leaders in similar ways to clinicians. How do we do this in an authentic and effective way? While imperturbability is essential for doctors, Sokol advocates for an "outward calm, a reassuring coolness" that inspires confidence—he contrasts it with empathy stating that "doctors crying in front of patients, praying with them, or displaying outward effusions of emotion" is not appropriate.

"Double Loop Learning in Organizations" by Chris Argyris (Argyris, 1977). This lengthy *Harvard Business Review* article is from 1977, clearly written at a time when leaders did not have to answer hundreds of e-mails per day and were pressured for time. But it is worth the effort as it explains well why we often fail to report failures! The HBR article includes many exciting nuggets, some of them particularly resonated with me, such as "… many people are struggling to counteract these processes of organizational rigidity and deterioration, especially at upper levels. In our society, executives work overtime and employees work the regular hours."

"One of the most toxic mixtures in a leader is a lack of self-doubt,
compounded by an unreflective conviction of one's rightness and
potential greatness, sometimes disguised under a cloak of manipulative
charm and, at its worst, leavened by aggression."
Em. Prof. Janice Reid AC at the 6th National Higher Education Women's
Leadership Summit 2015

Be Helpful

"The value of our lives is not determined by what we do for ourselves. The value of our lives is determined by what we do for others."
Simon Sinek, a British-born American author and motivational speaker

Everyone wants to be helpful, but when you enter an academic career, you are often told that you need to learn to say no. I strongly disagree with this all too familiar dictum. Adam Grant is the youngest-tenured and highest-rated professor at Wharton School of Business of the University of Pennsylvania (Grant, 2020) and an organizational psychologist who tries to bring social science into the workplace. I try to model Grant's undiscriminating helpfulness that reaps enormous professional benefits when you interact with many people. Essentially, Grant helps everyone who asks him for help, which is kind of an amazing concept. The best ideas occur to people who are touching multiple worlds and domains, something that most universities' strategic plans explicitly spell out, but that is rarely operationalized when research and teaching rankings of departments or disciplines result in competitive resource allocations. Being helpful can overcome these barriers as you create personal relationships that bind individuals despite organizational or financial disincentives to collaboration.

Susan Dominus writes in a 2013 *New York Times Magazine* about Grant that people like him are "strategic in their giving—they give to other givers and matchers, so that their work has the maximum desired effect; they give in ways that reinforce their social ties; and they consolidate their giving into chunks, so that the impact is intense enough to be gratifying" (Dominus, 2013).

Does this mean you have to do everything when asked? Of course not! But you can always try to connect requesters to people who are more suitable than yourself—like people who have more time and might need a nudge from you to collaborate. In my view, a flat out "No" to requests brings you nowhere.

I try to model Adam Grant's undiscriminating helpfulness, but admit it is often hard when you still need to answer e-mails after hours instead of just deleting them. But, generally speaking, I never say no to genuine requests for help.

Being helpful can mean a lot of things, including making people feel appreciated by, for instance, tapping into their wisdom and expertise, or running committees in a way that makes the best use of everyone's time. While these examples of helpfulness appear a bit self-centered, we should not forget that as academic leaders we are helpful when allowing everyone to work toward their full potential instead of loading them with administrative tasks. Only then can your academics advance their careers and have a fulfilling research and teaching career.

Mentoring

One way of helping others in a strategic manner is acting as a formal or informal mentor to early career academics. Given that we all have received advice during our careers, for me, this is also a form of paying back by sharing my knowledge and experience. We need to leave our organizations, and by extension the world, in a better position than we found it. One way of doing this is by mentoring the next generation of academic leaders. While I write these lines, I have just attended the Grand Finale of the 2020 Mentoring Program organized by Franklin Women, a community of women working in health and medical research related careers. Franklin Women aims to bring together like-minded women to create opportunities for networking, personal and professional development, and career progression, both in and outside of academia. During this 6-month program, I mentored a female biomedical researcher who is on a steep upward trajectory and hopefully benefitted from some external guidance. During the closing session, she said, "I look forward to the continuing mentorship from Heiko and hope that I continue to grow on the right leadership path." I have included her statement here to hopefully inspire readers to think how they can get involved in mentoring—in being helpful—as it is certainly a rewarding experience.

I have continued an informal mentoring relationship with my mentees after the completion of formal mentorship programs, meeting them semiregularly. I think that informal mentoring relationships can be very effective, but especially for early career academics and professionals, I believe that kicking off the process during a formal program can provide a supportive environment for the start of a long-term mentor–mentee relationship.

Selecting the right mentor–mentee pairs is the crucial step in any mentoring engagement—a role that is often taken on by academic leaders. I feel very strongly that mentors should not be in the chain of command and conversely that, as a leader, you should never engage in a mentoring relationship with one of your direct or indirect reports. As leaders in our universities we have, of course, the obligation to help each academic to advance their career and help them to grow, but this should not be confused with mentoring. I have had first-hand experience during my career how well-meaning advice from a mentor and supervisor can stifle career advancement as, for instance, leaving an organization to meet new challenges can benefit the mentee, but conflicts with the goals of the organization the mentor is supposed to advance.

How do we suggest mentor–mentee pairs? Any mentor–mentee relationship should be complementary, meaning, both should not have the same domain expertise (if the mentee is a scholar of logistics, she knows enough about logistics). Engaging with someone from a similar but slightly different domain will open new worlds for the mentee and help her to see things through a different lens. An appropriate career-advancement distance is also needed as the mentor should be above the mentee's level of advancement, but not too far removed. For instance, someone who became professor 20 years ago has often had a vastly different experience in advancing their career compared to someone being at postdoc level now. Advice might not be as helpful as it should be, or even misleading in the extreme.

I also find it helpful to demarcate what is not part of a mentoring relationship. For once, it is not coaching, or the teaching of a specific skill (Note that some people use the term "coaching" to describe what I call "mentoring"). Atul Gawande writes eloquently in his 2011 *The New Yorker* article about coaching. "No matter how well-trained people are, few can sustain their best performance on their own. That is where coaching comes in" (Gawande, 2011).

In addition, being a mentor is not taking someone under your patronage. Helping a protégé to meet important people and get invited could overlap with the role of a mentor but is not the core function of a mentor. Lastly, should formal mentors be paid, or should such a relationship always be unpaid? The answer to this question sits of course with the mentor who will need to determine if they charge or not. I have seen formal mentors deciding about compensation based on who pays for it. For instance, when an institution requests mentoring services for their leaders, often an hourly compensation is negotiated and paid by the institution directly to the mentor. Often, the mentor will reduce the hourly fees after the formal institutional mentorship relationship has ended and the mentee becomes self-paying (if so desired). Many mentors want to give back and provide their time for free, but this obviously depends on the circumstances of the mentor. It should never be assumed that services are free outside one's own organization.

Peer Support

Another, often overlooked, aspect of helpfulness is to support each other as leaders. All of us have peers, even if we are the top leader of our academic unit. There are always similar ones that are not in competition with our own and it is permissible to exchange ideas and solve common problems with their top leaders. When I started my leadership journey in Sydney, I was first appointed as deputy dean of the then Faculty of Dentistry. Not long after my arrival, I learned that there were deputy deans in each of the health faculties who then formed a "Deputy Deans Club." We met regularly from then on and learned from each other, discussed the upcoming organizational changes that would eventually affect us all in a very similar manner. Many of us still interact on a regular basis, and several are now in top leadership positions in our or other institutions.

Helpfulness comes in many disguises and here is probably a good place to pause and to note that the value in such close-knit leadership communities lies not just in being helpful and supportive, as important as this is, but in creating a "challenge network." What I mean by "challenge network" is a safe environment in which you can ask what you could have done better in certain situations and get an honest answer that neither hurts nor feels contrived. We are supposed to be innovative and come up with many strategic initiatives, but we need to remind ourselves that the more creative we are the more likely we are to develop bad ideas. Who will tell us that one of our new ideas is a bad one?

Contemporary workplace culture has adopted praise of staff as the key motivational tool to encourage performance improvement; however, this has resulted in a lack of critical appraisal of less-than-optimal performance. Most of us have been selected as academic leaders because of our outstanding research and teaching performance, or at least we hope so, which means we have, on average, received less critique than the average person. Now in our leadership positions, we will find very few staff members reporting to us having the courage to let us know if we made a mistake or displayed a shortcoming that should be addressed. The higher you are up the less often you will be directly observed by your boss resulting again in a reduction of critical feedback. If you do not actively seek critical feedback from a "challenge network" of trusted peers your perception of your performance might get skewed.

The concept of helpfulness and peer support is beautifully captured by Farid Muna and Ned Mansour who write about three leadership lessons that we can learn from Canada geese: "The first lesson is: work as a team: Canada Geese migrate long distances flying in V-formation. This formation results in lesser wind resistance, which allows the whole flock to add around 70 percent greater flying range than if each bird flew alone. Geese find out quickly that it pays handsomely to be team players. Second, wise leadership: when the leader at the apex of the V gets tired, it is relieved by another goose. Leaders rotate, empower, delegate, and even step down when it is in the best interest of the team. How often do we see this taking place among organizational leaders? Wise leaders ensure that their followers are well trained and developed to achieve true empowerment and smooth succession processes. Third, humane behavior: if a goose drops to the ground when it gets hurt or sick, two of its colleagues go down with it to take care of it until it either gets healthier or dies. In this fast-paced and competitive age, we seldom see managers going out of their way to help colleagues who are in trouble. In organizations, morale, productivity, and loyalty increase when employees are treated humanely" (Muna & Mansour, 2011).

Overcome Failure

We need to face the consequences of failure, our own ones, those of our team and failures experienced by individual staff members for whom we are responsible. Serious work includes taking risk—work is not wall-to-wall awesomeness. Helping staff who experienced failure is part of our role as academic leaders. We need to acknowledge that failure is a natural part of work. If an academic cannot tell you when they have failed during their career, the only logical conclusion is that they never tried anything that was challenging or never set an aspirational research goal.

We need to learn from these experiences. A recent article by Arthur Brooks in *The Atlantic* says that "[s]cholars who recently reviewed the careers of applicants for research-grant funding from the National Institutes of Health found that those who had been narrowly rejected early in their careers went on to outperform, in the long run, those who enjoyed early success." When reflecting on the many resumes that I have read during my career, I have not often read about failed grant applications in all but very early career academics' narrative.

How can we be helpful as leaders in this context? We can encourage risk taking and deal with the inevitable failures along the path, like a toddler exploring her environment ending up with bruised knees. Or we can act like helicopter parents hovering over the "toddler" to prevent any scratches. In my mind, nobody has expressed this dichotomy better than Jonathan Haidt and Greg Lukianoff in their book *The Coddling of the American Mind: How Good Intentions and Bad Ideas Are Setting Up a Generation for Failure*, which is applicable to all Western cultures and not limited to the United States as the title seems to imply (Lukianoff & Haidt, 2015).

Being helpful as an academic leader does not mean to prevent failure but overcoming it as the subheading of this section tries to imply. A similar thought was raised by David Brooks in *The Road to Character* "Among the privileged, especially the privileged young, you see people who have been raised to be approval-seeking machines. They may be active, busy, and sleepless, but inside they often feel passive and not in control. Their lives are directed by other people's expectations, external criteria, and definitions of success that don't actually fit them" (Brooks, 2015b). As academic leaders, we need to make our academics happier, so they are more productive and not fearful about a potential failure. Thus, it is vital to learn how to deal with failure even if you yourself never fail (hard to believe!), or if you cope well with the disappointment. Arthur Brooks states that people are increasingly more afraid of failure not just because of their overprotective Baby Boomer parents, but because "[s]ocial media threatens to make every slip-up an extinction-level event, socially and professionally." On the other hand, we should not encourage our staff to become fearless because "fearlessness is abnormal, and even dangerous, because it leads to foolish risk taking and bad leadership. Courage, on the other hand, helps you to balance prudence and resolve, even if the only thing you're defusing is an office conflict."

Disappointing as it is, nobody seems to have figured out the silver-bullet solution about how to deal with failure. I think that discussing potential failure with staff, being transparent about the risks and also admitting your own mistakes can help to pave the road to healthy risk taking that will reap rewards for your organization. It is easily said that "We learn from our mistakes. When we screw up and fail, we learn how not to handle things. We learn what not to do." and "If we don't practice failing, we can only safely fly on sunny days" (Parrish, 2022d).

Committees

Running committees is one of the key tasks for most (all?) academic leaders. As it is a key activity, there is also tremendous potential to be helpful in this role beyond your own sphere of influence in the university hierarchy. While I have yet to find a single person, who does not complain about their time being taken up by too many committee meetings, little effort has been devoted to teaching leaders how to run efficient and effective meetings. As stated above, this in my view, falls under the Lesson 3: "Be Helpful" because your team will appreciate you running committees in a way that makes them feel that you value their time, their input, their independence, and their expertise. Before engaging in any committee work, it might be helpful, from an organizational perspective, to perform an inventory of all committees. This is a great way to figure out how many committees operate, what they are covering, and if there is any duplication or unwarranted overlap. Are they all still needed? Who is on those committees? Once we have established a committee is needed, here are a few basics that may sound trivial but that I daily see not properly applied.

Preparing a Meeting: Committee meetings should be prepared. One would think that is obvious, but how often have you sat in a meeting where you wondered how many minutes, or seconds, has the committee chair thought about this meeting in advance. Being inclusive, and trying to minimize "administrivia," starts for me with the agenda which I make available for editing for almost all meetings that I am running. Today, this can be accomplished in so many ways that I cannot list them all here, but from Google Docs to Microsoft Teams or Evernote, most platforms allow you to give others edit access. As chair, I set up a scaffolding agenda and then encourage members of the committee to contribute to the agenda—even last-minute additions are welcome. This works for all meetings that do not follow very strict governing rules, such as mandatory distribution of the agenda in advance.

Providing Structure: Often, I try to include at the top of the agenda pack the vision, purpose, mission, or strategy that drives this committee, as a tacit reminder why we are actually coming together. It is critical to separate items for discussion, items for decisions and items for noting in advance—each topic followed by an approximation of how much time it will take up during the meeting to set expectations for the meeting itself, but also for how members should prepare. While I personally hate agenda packs that include hundreds of pages for noting, I am not (yet) ready to exert energy to fight about items for noting as they can be ignored if not important. My efforts focus on which discussion and, even more importantly, which decision items are supporting the strategy. Everything that is not supporting the strategy or is operational gets cut out or pushed to the "For Noting" section.

Running the Meeting: Starting a meeting will set the tone for the rest of the meeting and you want to choose wisely if you want to employ a more formal or more informal tone. Usually, you want to start with some housekeeping items, like asking if someone must declare a new Conflict of Interest given the agenda items. Often, this is followed by a short discussion about new threats or problems facing the realm of the committee, followed by an update from the committee chair about topics that have been discussed in the governing body that sits above the committee in the organizational hierarchy if this is appropriate. Then, you want to delve into the main items for discussion and decision. These should make up most of the meeting time which should never exceed more than 90 minutes in total. I am aware that some people think that they must run multi-hour meetings. But in my opinion, most people cannot concentrate beyond 90 minutes resulting in a reduced gradually deteriorating meeting effectiveness. During a workshop with the Australian Institute of Company Directors, I have heard the advice that each meeting should end with an evaluation of the meeting—I think this is a good idea, but I use this technique only occasionally, sometimes formally during the meeting and other times informally when I subsequently meet with individual committee members for other reasons. Many readers have heard the term "Minimal Viable Product (MVP)" which is often used in the company start-up world for a version of a product with enough features to be usable by some testers who can then provide feedback to the development team to potentially avoid lengthy and unnecessary work. The same concept can be used when running meetings by asking yourself what the "Minimal Viable Governance (MVG)" is needed to be effective and efficient to avoid lengthy and unnecessary committee work.

Herding the Cats: I believe that committee members, including the chair, should always feel a bit uncomfortable during a meeting. This does not mean you want to make people feel miserable, but that you should not engage in formulaic work. Instead, focus on the items that are problematic and do not have easy solutions.

If something could have been easily resolved in advance of the meeting, you, as chair, should have done so already and just note the decision in the "For Noting" section. Invariably, you will have committee members who try to derail your carefully prepared agenda by bringing up tangential items, attempting to self-promote or trying to push their own agenda. Your role as the one running the meeting is to prevent this from happening without being rude—remember the Lesson 1: "Be Nice." There are several techniques that I have successfully used, including "Thanks for this suggestion! We will talk about xyz during our March meeting." or "Let us discuss this one offline" or "I suggest that we delegate this task to xyz" or "Let us park this for later discussion."

Decision Making: It is important that you send signals from the start how you would like to make decisions during the meeting. If you, as chair, state your opinion and ask if anyone has an issue with your decision, you will most likely not get many members to offer dissenting opinions. But this does not mean you need to resort to secret voting on paper ballots. A rather useful method is described in Daniel Kahneman's book *Thinking, Fast and Slow*: "before an issue is discussed, all members of the committee should be asked to write a very brief summary of their position. This procedure makes good use of the value of the diversity of knowledge and opinion in the group. The standard practice of open discussion gives too much weight to the opinions of those who speak early and assertively, causing others to line up behind them" (Kahneman, 2013). I think that genuine discussion can spin off from this exercise. You also want to signal to the committee members that they all have an important task and responsibility which will require higher-level thinking. That, of course, requires that you have something complicated to decide when you meet. As this might not always be the case, feel empowered to cancel a meeting, acknowledging that everyone is busy, and substitute it with an electronic distribution of the items for noting. Believe me, no one will complain. Nothing is worse than a meeting without a larger purpose! While you do not want to preempt decisions, you might want to start summarizing the discussion to date, add any new points and determine what is not negotiable. Then, open for a broad discussion reminding all members that they have been selected to have a voice. While I talk in Lesson 6: "Think and Work Strategically" about importance versus urgency, the same applies for meeting: important decisions need to be made before urgent ones.

Too Many Meetings

While committees have meetings, this subheading is about "just meetings" instead of formal gatherings of committee members to make decisions. The

COVID-19 crisis has resulted in an unprecedented increase in meetings (total time spent in meetings and number of meetings) as evidenced in quantitative research by Microsoft (Iqbal, 2022). New technologies allow us to invite people to meetings regardless of their location, even disregarding the time zone in which they live or their work–life balance. Because it is easy and seemingly cost-free, we put little thought into the meeting's effectiveness. Think a few decades back: I am sure if a university president would have called a meeting requiring ten leaders from various regional campuses to travel to the main campus, providing accommodations and catering for the attendees, just to do weekly chitchats about minor decisions and to prevent attendees from reading lengthy documents by themselves, this president would have had an interesting conversation with members of the university's governing body.

The important question is of course not about effort but about outcomes: Has our relentless commitment to ever more meetings increased our productivity? Are we being helpful as academic leaders when we gather our team members for a meeting instead of letting them do their research and teaching?

The result of too many meetings is often that nobody takes good notes. The next meeting is just around the corner, during which attendees can update each other about what has been forgotten. Nowadays, only top university executives have the luxury of a personal assistant (PA) who could take notes. Thus, not going to meetings is not an option, because you cannot learn sufficiently about crucial discussions from the brief minutes. Requesting to record a meeting one cannot attend, something that can be easily accomplished with online meetings, only increases the number of meetings for each individual. Now, you can also participate in important meetings that conflict with other important meetings using meeting recordings. If we pursue the record-for-listen-later approach we would be able to bring everyone's productivity down to zero.

Some companies are experimenting with AI-based transcriptions of recorded meetings. However, I wonder about the dynamics of meetings with retrospective surveillance, given that everyone can later search and read everything that has been said. Others might have different attitudes to ubiquitous meeting recordings—any surveillance gives me unease after growing up in East Germany. In addition, will, then, university executives just skip meetings and just read the transcript afterward and therefore not contribute ideas to the discussion?

Leaders should ask themselves first, why are we meeting; or to be more precise, why do specific topics end up on meeting agendas? Unfortunately, the answer to this question is too often one of the following:

- We know that most people don't read long memos, policies, guidelines, or plans. Thus, we help staff by presenting what has been sent around but has not been read. Once your team members have spent weekend hours reading the material that you sent around only to listen to it again during the Monday meeting, they will quickly cease to read anything in advance. Who is to blame them?
- The presenter has promised her superior that she will consult with the group represented in a particular meeting. No goal can be articulated for the presentation as it is purely For Your Information (FYI) to tick the box "Consultation with XYZ completed."
- Compliance problems with a particular policy at the lowest level of the hierarchy have resulted in the need to "do something" about the "unacceptable situation." Instead of a thoughtful (time-consuming!) analysis of the barriers to compliance, a presentation (quickly done!) about the policy to middle managers is arranged. However, this particular audience is mostly aware of the policy.

So, what can we do as leaders to empower our teams to get some work done during work hours? Thompson writes in *The Atlantic* that published research data by Microsoft reveal emerging productivity patterns of knowledge workers who now have a third peak of productivity later in the evening (Thompson, 2022). Anecdotally, I see the same happening in academic institutions which is clearly detrimental to any work–life balance. Thompson attributes some of this trend to the use of technology for work and home: "As work becomes more like life, it also becomes more of life." He reflects on meeting culture, quoting Microsoft's Mary Czerwinski, "People have 250 percent more meetings every day than they did before the pandemic …That means everything else—like coding and e-mail and writing—is being pushed later." Thompson says, "Meetings require synchronicity: Everybody be present now. But most white-collar labor can be at least somewhat asynchronous."

We need to help our staff by deciding "what work must be synchronous (meetings) and what work can be asynchronous (emails or shared docs)" so that they get their evenings back. I don't think that there is an easy answer to this question! The development of a common understanding of the challenges in the workplace and finding suitable solutions for them is not just a question of finding the most efficient way of communication, but also on what is best for the team at this moment. For instance, if there has been conflict among team members about a certain decision, e-mail might be an efficient way to communicate about the topic, but is it the best way to restore the team's cohesiveness?

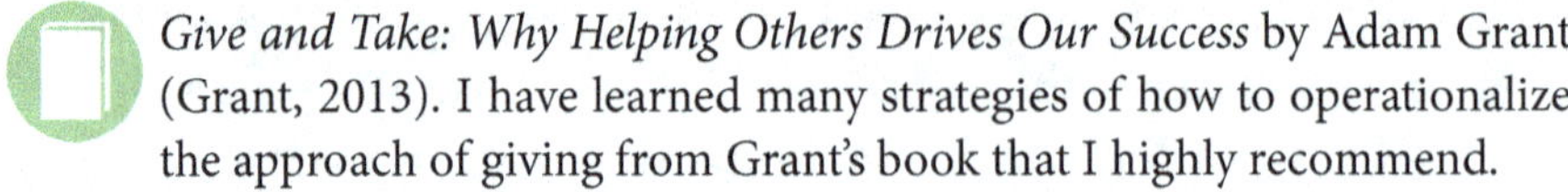

Give and Take: Why Helping Others Drives Our Success by Adam Grant (Grant, 2013). I have learned many strategies of how to operationalize the approach of giving from Grant's book that I highly recommend.

"Is Giving the Secret to Getting Ahead?" by Susan Dominus (Dominus, 2013). If a book is too long for you, try this already mentioned 2013 *The New York Times Magazine* article that reminds us that "tirelessly helping others could be the key to hyper-efficiency."

Understanding Humans in the Wild - A Conversation with Adam Grant by Sam Harris (Harris, 2019). If you like Adam Grant's book or the article mentioned above, or if you want to make up your mind if you should read the book, Sam Harris' podcast will help you by listening to a conversation with Grant about the social science of the workplace, including how teams work effectively, the nature of power, personality types and fundamental styles of interaction, the critical skill of saying no, and other topics.

"Top athletes and singers have coaches. Should you?" by Atul Gawande (Gawande, 2011). Gawande eloquently writes about mentoring and coaching in his 2011 *The New Yorker* article: "No matter how well-trained people are, few can sustain their best performance on their own. That is where coaching comes in."

"Leadership lessons from Canada geese" by Farid A. Muna and Ned Mansour (Muna & Mansour, 2011). I cite parts of the abstract of this article in this lesson, but it is certainly worthwhile to read the entire article that uses this wonderful analogy to teach us all some bird stories.

Board meeting agenda by the Australian Institute of Company Directors (AICD) (Australian Institute of Company Directors, 2017). This is just one of many helpful tools and tips available at the AICD website. Just use "board" and "director" as synonyms for "committee" and "member" and you will find a wealth of resources that help you to become a better committee chair.

"Remote work doesn't work, if you don't rethink meetings" by Mike Walsh (Walsh, 2020a). Having talked about chairing meetings in this chapter requires us to reflect on our new way of meeting—via video conferencing. Walsh asks in his article what it takes to run a good virtual meeting. Technical aspects are important, but what really counts are how to successfully manage a distributed workforce and have the right meeting culture.

"Google X and the Science of Radical Creativity. How the secretive Silicon Valley lab is trying to resurrect the lost art of invention" by Derek Thompson (Thompson, 2017). This article about X, Alphabet's Moonshot factory, explores how leaders should deal with failed ideas. I acknowledge that the article is helpful but far from conclusive.

"There is a special place in hell for morally indifference and neutrality." Dante Alighieri (1265–1321), Italian poet, writer, and philosopher

Build Resilience

"Most people are neither for you nor against you; they are thinking about themselves."
David Brooks, political and cultural commentator for
The New York Times (Brooks, 2015a)

Building resilience is clearly desirable and something we all should aspire to in our personal and professional lives. However, the question is how should we do this? A good start is to change our mindset by accepting that work is not "wall-to-wall awesomeness" (Klosterman, 2014), but that your role as academic leader is to answer the question, "What am I doing to ensure that my staff enjoy working here producing excellent research and deliver outstanding teaching that changes the lives of our students?" When in a good mood, people become more intuitive and more creative as Nobel Prize winner Daniel Kahneman has scientifically proven (Kahneman, 2013). There is even a Resilience Institute that helps leaders and teams to increase their resilience—I am not sure about their 60-factor resilience assessment app including 55 micro-learning videos and an AI chatbot for daily tactical calm sessions, but given that they have been in business for almost 20 years shows the importance of the topic (*The Resilience Institute*, 2020). The Institute defines resilience as "the learned ability to demonstrate bounce, courage, connection and creativity." They asked more than 26,000 professionals over a period of six years and reported in 2016 that 55% of professionals worry excessively, 45% experience distress symptoms, 35% are unable to relax and 30% experience excessive work intensity. The problem is that we as leaders must be seen as caring about our culture and the resilience of our staff and not just simply tick a box as our duty of care.

A McKinsey Health Institute article resonated with me as it cites research that many employers, and I would add universities here, "have responded by investing more into mental health and well-being than ever before. … Many companies offer a host of wellness benefits such as yoga, meditation app subscriptions, well-being days, and training sessions on time management and productivity. In fact, it is estimated that nine in ten organizations around the world offer some form of wellness program." Recognizing the importance of well-being is a positive first step. However, the article continues that "many employers focus on individual-level interventions that remediate symptoms, rather than resolve the causes of employee burnout. Employing these types of interventions may lead employers to overestimate the impact of their wellness programs and benefits and to underestimate the critical role of the workplace in reducing burnout and supporting employee mental health and well-being" (Brassey et al., 2022).

Personal Resilience

Making failure and vulnerability acceptable without fostering mediocracy however remains a challenge for most leaders. Thus, let's start with our own resilience. Nobody expressed the personal aspects of resilience better than John Gardner, secretary of Health, Education, and Welfare under President Lyndon Johnson: "The things you learn in maturity aren't simple things such as acquiring information and skills. You learn not to engage in self-destructive behavior. You learn not to burn up energy in anxiety. You discover how to manage your tensions. You learn that self-pity and resentment are among the most toxic of drugs. You find that the world loves talent but pays off on character. You come to understand that most people are neither for you nor against you; they are thinking about themselves. You learn that no matter how hard you try to please, some people in this world are not going to love you, a lesson that is at first troubling and then really quite relaxing" (Brooks, 2015a).

How do we balance openness, transparency, and honesty with our roles as leaders? Steve Simpson and Stef du Plessis, employee engagement experts, say in their book, *A Culture Turned*, "A single toxic comment from a senior leader can undo weeks, months, or even years of team building" (Simpson & Du Plessis, 2015). As a leader you can create a negative 'unwritten ground rule' that undermines an otherwise positive workplace culture. Or, as we say in Germany with less verbal dexterity, "The fish starts to stink from the head." In other words, as leaders we influence the people around us. This is common sense, but it is also scientifically sound as we, as human beings, are social animals which means that our "brains naturally and unconsciously mimic the moods of those around us, particularly people we spend a great deal of time with. This neuronal mirroring is the basis for our ability to feel empathy" (Bradberry, 2016). But this also results in us triggering negative thinking in the people around us which is not good for our brains as it rewires our neurons for complaining.

The rise of political populism has also resulted in a "general proclivity to be a criticizer rather than a doer and to tear down rather than build up," says John Halamka, president of the Mayo Clinic Platform, and implores that we as leaders should swim against this tide: "Let's all be doers. Our position will be imperfect because there will always be room for improvement" (Halamka, 2015b).

We also should remind ourselves and our staff that the harder it gets the better we usually perform as a team, a university, and a nation. While no one suggests we should embrace war or disaster, these times of hardship bring people together. I have seen this first-hand when I lived in the United States when the September 11, 2001 terrorist attacks happened. In a country where political dialogue is hard to achieve among politicians and people who mostly fall into one of two camps, suddenly a sense of unity befell most people stripping away the deeply ingrained differences. Evolutionary speaking, groups of humans had to help each other to survive and the harder the conditions the more they had to help each other. Junger argues in his book *Tribe: On Homecoming and Belonging* that modern society reduces the need for helping each other and being resilient (Junger, 2016). Nowadays, only disasters and war create the need to work together which improves the sense of belonging and increases resilience. How can we make use of this as leaders? Clearly, we do not want to create disaster to improve the resilience and mental health of our staff. However, creating a sense of urgency and being honest about challenges that the team is facing will bring people together and this sense of community improves mental health and resilience according to Junger.

Mindfulness

Many leaders complain that these are unprecedented times, brought upon them by a global pandemic, a war in Europe, technological advances, global competitive markets, Artificial Intelligence, social media and much more. These challenges force leaders to be more reactive and allow less room for being proactive. Clearly, there is more pressure in modern times than there was in the past. We also need to acknowledge that we humans still run-on monkey software as descendants of primates—no hardware upgrade in 160,000 years. A tiger charging toward you requires an immediate reaction without much deeper thinking if you do not want to become a meal. On the contrary, responding instantly to a verbal challenge in a meeting without much thinking might end your career. What do I do to prevent me from reacting too fast when faced by another challenge? For several decades, every day, I have been practicing mindfulness in the morning—long before the rise of "Mac-Mindfulness" that can now be found everywhere. Long-time practitioners of mindfulness may practice 20 minutes each day, but even 5 minutes a day can make a world of difference. I think (hope) that it has made a positive effect on regulating my emotions by rewriting my emotional software. As I write in Lesson 1: "Be Nice," controlling your emotions gives you more degrees of freedom. Resilience has to do with the effect that the behavior of others has on us. If we are angry, we can decide how long we want to be locked up in this mental state. Self-awareness gives us the power to reduce this feeling from days to 30 seconds which really gives you superpowers. Sam Harris writes, "If you think that you can stay angry for a day or even an hour without continually manufacturing this emotion by thinking without knowing that you are thinking, you are mistaken. This is an objective claim about the mechanics of your subjectivity. You can learn not to stay angry. … Almost everyone you meet is practically drowning in self-concern. Just look at them. They are broadcasting their own self-doubt and anxiety and disappointment. You are surrounded by a carnival of human frailty. So, compassion is available. We are all on the Titanic together. This might sound depressing, but the flip side is also true. This brief life together is a beautiful miracle. This is the only circumstance that exists to be enjoyed. This is the only life you have so you might enjoy it" (Harris, 2014). I have learned to understand that most suffering is not coming from other people but comes from the inside—an inside for which we are responsible ourselves. Many people see a psychoanalyst to talk about their problems and I am sure it helps them, but Matthieu Ricard, a Buddhist monk and the French interpreter for the Dalai Lama, notes that "constant rumination is one of the main symptoms of depression. What we need is to gain freedom from the mental chain reactions that rumination endlessly perpetuates. One should learn to let thoughts arise and be freed to go as soon as they arise, instead of letting them invade one's mind" (Ricard & Singer, 2017). While psychoanalysis seems to encourage rumination by exploring the intricacies of one's mental confusion and self-centeredness, meditation is the opposite—learning how to escape negative emotions and feelings. I like Ricard's analogy "… when we encounter severe difficulties that require fast solutions, such as a complicated traffic situation. We immediately call on a large repertoire of escape strategies that we have learned and practiced, and then we choose among them without much reasoning, relying mainly on subconscious heuristics. Apparently, if we are not experienced with contemplative practice, we haven't gone through the driving school for the management of emotional conflicts" (Ricard & Singer, 2017).

Tim Ireland writes in *Scientific American*, "MRI scans show that after an eight-week course of mindfulness practice, the brain's 'fight or flight' center, the amygdala, appears to shrink. This primal region of the brain, associated with fear and emotion, is involved in the initiation of the body's response to stress. As the amygdala shrinks, the pre-frontal cortex—associated with higher order brain functions such as awareness, concentration and decision-making—becomes thicker" (Ireland, 2014). While my goal is certainly not to be less empathetic or appear cold-blooded, decreased emotional activity allows me to be the calmest person in the room during heated discussion. In addition, I believe (maybe wishful thinking?) that meditation has helped me to increase focus to get more work done in less time.

Personal Well-being

How do I cope with the demands of my role? To be resilient, my mantra is Family comes first! My family is a continuous responsibility. I am a father and husband and son $24 \times 7 \times 365$. But as leaders we also need to take care of ourselves and our own emotional and physical well-being. That means we need to take real leave, not one during which we constantly check e-mail and take phone calls. I am aware that this is easier said than done and I am guilty of checking e-mail during my annual leave. I have made a compromise with myself and my family to only engage in these work activities, online approvals, urgent e-mails, and the like, for a maximum of one hour per day when the rest of the family has nothing planned. While not ideal for many reasons, it reduces my anxiety of returning from a vacation to find my inbox overloaded while everyone is expecting me to be back on deck and fully responsive to new problems.

Another aspect of personal resilience building is how to best benefit from the relaxation during your annual leave. However, I often wonder how great it would be if someone would produce my widgets while I am on annual leave. But, like many other leaders, I don't make widgets and no actual strategic leadership task gets accomplished while I am on annual leave. And while some operational tasks have been completed while I am gone, most of the time, I see my vacation just as a deferral of tasks which results in overtime upon my return. Thus, the positive effect of relaxation and switching off is quickly wiped out by the many extra hours it takes to sift through hundreds of e-mails and progress strategic tasks that have been temporarily abandoned. Checking e-mail while on leave is one solution but is not good for your health—it seems so innocent on the surface, but a recent study found that being "reachable" raises cortisol levels (Basu, 2015).

One, admittingly partial, solution to the problem could be something that a fellow leader at my institution recently suggested to me. She shared that upon her return from leave, she advises her executive assistant to book for each week of leave a "laundry day." The idea is that, similar to doing laundry after unpacking your suitcases, you clean up the accumulated mess at your desk during these days. You are back from leave, you are working, but you don't start your usual routine of meetings and other commitments for a few days. You can even keep your out-of-office message on for these "laundry days." It works wonders for your well-being, and you will retain the positive effects of annual leave for a longer period.

Resilient Attitude

There is another attitude that can reduce stress and increase resilience. I have adopted John Halamka's point about managing up that emphasizes that 10-20% of our work life is spent on non-value-added activities, such as standing meetings that may not be relevant to my area (Halamka, 2015a). However, attending these meetings is important for my school or the larger organization, such as the faculty or my university. While such obligations interrupt my "real" work and creativity, I have succeeded in convincing myself that investing this time is required by my institution and might (I am really optimistic here!) pay dividends over time. I have decided not to get worked up about these obligations, which is calming.

Most of what we do in leadership roles is solving problems. If you think back, you will have to acknowledge that most past problems were of a nature that you could deal with and solve. Thus, the first conclusion should be that current problems are of the same nature, meaning they have a solution. The second conclusion you should draw is that problems will always arise—so better learn to enjoy or at least live with them. Or did you expect to wake up one day and find there are no problems and an empty e-mail inbox? Do you want nothing on your to-do list? We tacitly assume we can solve all the problems and avoid any new ones. The expectation that there will be no more problems and then subsequent disappointment when there are new ones is a source of much suffering (Harris, 2020c). Russel Ackoff goes a step further and describes the problem-solving role for managers and leaders as follows: "Managers are not confronted with problems that are independent of each other, but with dynamic situations that consist of complex systems of changing problems that interact with each other. I call such situations messes …. Managers do not solve problems, they manage messes" (Ackoff et al., 2007).

I believe that once we become resilient ourselves, we have a much better chance to instill resilience into our staff. Stress reduction can be achieved via physical exercise, and we can, and I believe should, also exercise our minds with meditation. We can also start by incorporating resilience attributes into the recruitment process by asking how applicants have dealt with a major work crisis or personal crisis. If an applicant claims that he or she never experienced a crisis, then this candidate should probably not be on your shortlist. We can make it known that we expect peak performance from everyone while acknowledging that peak performance is not the same as sustainable performance. Lastly and probably most importantly, we as leaders should encourage staff to speak up about their own struggles and then show compassion by acknowledging our own weaknesses and mistakes.

Culture Change

Changing the culture of any kind of organization is hard, requiring resilience of the leader. Academic leaders are not approaching their role with a just-getting-the-job-done attitude, but one that embraces creativity and innovation which drives the organizations forward. Gary Pisano, Professor of Business Administration at Harvard Business School, reflects on how we display tolerance for failure while not permitting incompetence in his article titled "The Hard Truth About Innovative Cultures: Creativity can be messy. It needs discipline and management" (Pisano, 2019).

Often culture change means for the academic leader to stop some high-visibility projects that have been supported by past leaders. A hard task as we are often struggling when telling a team that, despite their best efforts and past encouragement, the project in which they have invested hard work and to which they are emotionally attached, will be terminated. Why is this? Maybe it starts already in school when educators favor less creative children "because people who are more creative also tend to be more playful, unconventional, and unpredictable, and all of this makes them harder to control. No matter how much we say we value creation, deep down, most of us value control more. And so we fear change and favor familiarity. Rejecting is a reflex." (Ashton, 2015).

In contrast, Pisano writes, "Psychological safety is an organizational climate in which individuals feel they can speak truthfully and openly about problems without fear of reprisal." Our, understandable, desire to achieve consensus on decisions is often counter to such a climate. "Fail fast! Fail often!" sounds nice, but the truth is that, financially and psychologically, failure sucks (Thompson, 2017). In most organizations, projects that don't work out are stigmatized, and their staff are reprimanded. Derek Thompson writes in his exposé of Google's moonshot factory in *The Atlantic* that X's leaders had "to build a unique emotional climate, where people are excited to take big risks despite the inevitability of…' falling flat on their face.' It is our role as leaders to achieve a climate in which it is permissible to fail without getting psychologically or career-wise damaged.

Pisano concludes that we face continuous challenges as leaders when we try to balance a "tolerance for failure [that] can encourage slack thinking and excuse making" and "can become permission to take poorly conceived risks" with an "overly strict discipline [that] can squash good but ill-formed ideas." While there is no magic formula for making the right decisions in these complicated situations, awareness and acknowledgment of these complexities can go a long way.

One way to distinguish the two, and most importantly explain the resulting decisions to your team, is to shift the discussion from failure to learning. A failure is acceptable if we have learned something that will help us succeed the next time around. A failed risky idea will provide lessons learned if properly executed and documented; sloppy thinking will not yield learning and just produce waste.

Related to this discussion is the issue of safetyism and how we deal with emotional safety that is increasingly perceived as under attack by views that claim that "speech is violence." More about this in Lesson 1: "Be Nice" and in Jonathan Haidt's and Greg Lukianoff's fiercely discussed book *The Coddling of the American Mind* (Haidt & Lukianoff, 2018).

Creativity in Hard Times

The science writer Matt Ridley, in conversation with Shane Parrish (Parrish, 2021), defined innovation as "the process by which a bright idea is turned into something practical, reliable and available and affordable for ordinary people." While I personally believe that fundamental research is important to bring humanity forward, such applied or translational thinking might help us as leaders to motivate our people during challenging times that are too often characterized in a negative way. I heard many pessimistic voices describing the COVID-19 pandemic and its economic and societal impact as the beginning of the end. Certainly, when we heard the news about the pandemic, or news about any other natural disasters and the economy at large, it was easy to become pessimistic about the future. How do we lead our teams out of such thinking that stifles innovation and creativity? Many focused on business-as-usual only without much drive for innovation and creativity. Matt says in his conversation with Shane that "innovation is unbelievably important. It's by far the biggest story of the last 500 years. It's the reason for optimism for the next 500 years, it's infinite." I agree with this sentiment and often use examples from Steven Pinker's book *The Better Angels of Our Nature* (Pinker, 2011) to show that we are in fact not the generation where everything turned from good to bad.

Matt makes another good point about innovation as it is fueled by collaboration and the spirit of sharing ideas "I think what happens is that people share their ideas, exchange their ideas, collaborate. And what really counts is how well people are communicating with each other, not how clever they are as individuals." One way for us is to ensure that people collaborate and connect to each other, inside our organizations, but also beyond. While this is easily said during times of constrained travel, the acceptance of zoom video calls and other online meeting platforms has given us the legitimacy to start collaborations without prior face-to-face meetings. While I still think that personal connections are important, they also limit the number of people you could potentially meet.

Further Readings

Thinking, Fast and Slow by Nobel Prize Winner Daniel Kahneman (Kahneman, 2013). The behavioral economist explains how we as humans make choices, from economic decisions, such as stratifying your investment portfolio, to very personal decisions, such as continuing with a diet. Understanding how our decisions are influenced by the prospect of regret and existing prejudices has helped me as a leader when having to deal with complex situations that require a nuanced response to deal with the subtle complexity of human judgment.

"The Problem With Meaning" by David Brooks (Brooks, 2015a) explains meaningfulness and self-regarding feelings in a short and concise way that helped me see self-preservation in a different light.

Waking Up by Sam Harris (Harris, 2020c). If you want to learn meditation, I highly recommend using this app by Sam Harris. If you think that just saying "Relax!" will do it, you are wrong. You can't just relax actively; mindfulness will help you to relax and build resilience.

The Road to Character by David Brooks (Brooks, 2015b) describes examples of extraordinary resilience by a diverse set of highly accomplished individuals. It is refreshing to read Brooks who brings the character development and leadership skill development to the forefront of the narrative. Instead of focusing on biographical details or family trees of famous people, Brooks describes how people rise to the occasion, and become great leaders in various spheres of life and at different periods. Some of the people he describes are severely flawed in character and display poor judgement, but they all eventually emerge as leaders. He describes their struggles to build a strong inner character.

"Never give up: never, never, never."
Winston Churchill (1874–1965), British statesman, army officer,
writer, prime minister of the UK from 1940 to 1945, during
World War II, and again from 1951 to 1955.

Enable Change

"We have a natural resistance to being told what is good for us."
John Updike (1932–2009), American novelist, poet, short-story
writer, art critic, and literary critic (Updike, 2009)

Impressions are remarkably perseverant. We all have experienced how hard it is to convince someone else to change his or her mind. I am writing these lines in the week after the 2020 U.S. presidential elections—probably there are very few better examples of a polarized political landscape to showcase how hard it is to convince the other side of the need to change. The political climate reinforces the idea that while knowledge is necessary to initiate change, it alone is not enough to persuade people to alter their beliefs, or, as Elizabeth Kolbert's *The New Yorker* calls it "Why Facts Don't Change Our Minds" (Kolbert, 2017). Kolbert cites several studies that show the human mind's limitations of acting based on reason, and while academics pride themselves on being driven by science, I suspect they are no exception here. Subjects in study after study have shown that after being told that an initial set of facts were false and misleading, they did not change their mind, something that has huge implications beyond the political arena.

As leaders, it is part of our role to change not only the opinion, and subsequently behavior, of one person, but of entire teams and sometimes even entire universities. Often these opinions, or ways of doing things, have been ingrained for years or even decades. You will learn the limitations of reason as you will find that it is hard to change the behavior of others, especially if you have a lot of intransigent academics to deal with. What can you do about this if evidence shows that facts are ignored? For me, it works when I tell stories—I believe that humans need a causal narrative—we are not built for reasoning by numbers or evidence as much as we like to think that we are. My own research on behavior change of healthcare providers has shown over and over again that knowledge is not a good target if you want to change behavior (O'Donnell et al., 2013). Richard Asher says about new ideas, here in a medical context but applicable everywhere, that they "are much easier to believe if they are comforting, and that many clinical notions are accepted because they are comforting rather than because there is any evidence to support them. Just as we swallow food because we like it not because of its nutritional content, so do we swallow ideas because we like them and not because of their rational content" (Asher, 1972).

There are hundreds (thousands?) of books and resources on change leadership, I list a few below, but the most important aspect in my view, is to recognize if the planned change is of technical nature or of what Heifetz calls adaptive nature (R. A. Heifetz & Linsky, 2017). If change is of technical nature, the problem is usually clearly defined and an expert familiar with contemporary practices will be able to determine the solution. As a leader, you often can convince others of the necessary change by either benchmarking to competitors or by inviting an expert group as an advisory team. The more challenging change is the adaptive one where not even the question is clearly defined. Here the solution and the implementation require new learning and your team members have responsibility for finding the solutions. Often during times of adaptive change, leaders need to think politically to forge alliances and accept that casualties and difficulties will be on the path to progress.

Organizations are obviously different, and I have seen leaders struggle when they join a large, established organization after having worked in a small agile one before, like coming from a start-up company to a huge research university. Newer and smaller organizations have a larger disruptive potential compared to older and larger ones. The reason is not a lack of competencies or assets but rather that established organizations face high opportunity costs and will therefore not be able to allocate sufficient resources to disruptive projects. In contrast, new entrants can get excited about a small niche market as they invest at an early point and gain momentum while the incumbents enter the new area when it is too late. A good example of this problem is the desire of universities to enter the micro-credentialing or non-award space—while small providers are generating significant revenue through online learning and small continuing professional development courses, many universities have established committees who are charged with thinking about how their institutions can establish themselves in this space.

Inevitable Change

I have read somewhere that a leader was once asked if you can lead without changing things. Her answer was threefold. First, from physics to biology and chemistry, from the micro to the macro, we know that the universe is constantly changing. So, no. Secondly, organizations are dynamic systems, constantly changing. So, no, once again. Thirdly, she asked, "Why would one want to lead without changing things?" No one should take a leadership position if she does not have a vision for making the situation, organization, society, etc. a better place. Laura Tingle puts it this way: "To be a leader … you either have to know what it is that you want to persuade other people to do, or else have the knack of identifying and synthesizing an issue on which people are seeking leadership. You also need to know how you are going to do something about such issues. And you have to know what the most important things are to get done at any given point of time. Then you have to make the rest of us understand why these things are important and what you are going to do about them" (Tingle, 2018).

Most leaders have completed various assessments of their leadership style inventorying their traits and characteristics, maybe via a formal external 360 process or an introspective Myers-Briggs Type Indicator (MBTI) tool. While some think that all these tools are biased and meaningless or that MBTI is "harmless and it provides a nice income for many consultants" (Hogan, 2007), I think that such assessments can be useful when done every 10 years or less frequently. I have had to conduct these assessments too often in various roles and feel that they become less useful for me each time as I know the results in advance, which might display my personal recalcitrance. What is, however, important when it comes to initiating change in an organization is that every leader should, what I would call, flex their leadership style. What do I mean by that? Some leaders are clearly more people-oriented with high scores in emotional intelligence who try to integrate diverse perspectives and strive to build interpersonal trust. Andrés Tapia, senior client partner at the global organizational consulting firm Korn Ferry, calls these leaders "heart-led leaders" (Tapia et al., 2020). Others are more action-oriented with high scores on flexibility and inquisitiveness trying to achieve transformations, Tapia calls these leaders "head-led leaders." Presumably, if you belong to one or the other you are already good at the traits that belong to your group which provides opportunity to develop expertise in the traits typically associated with the other. "Heart-centered leaders, for example, must develop an approach to diversity and inclusion that leads to organizational transformation. Head-centered leaders, meanwhile, could achieve transformation even more effectively, if they were to become more emotionally connected with the diversity of people they were leading" (Tapia et al., 2020).

In 1994, Ronald Heifetz, from the Kennedy School of Government at Harvard University, wrote a book called *Leadership Without Easy Answers*, in which he argues that leadership, power and formal authority too often get confused and need to be carefully distinguished. He defines leadership as helping a community embrace change (R. A. Heifetz, 1994). I also find, although controversial for many reasons, Cathy Fiorina's quote from her book *Tough Choices* inspiring: "Leadership is about a positive difference for and with others. Leadership is about integrity of one's character, the caliber of one's capabilities, and the effectiveness of one's collaboration with others" (Fiorina, 2007).

Change by Consensus

If you want to change something, you need to first be creative to develop an innovative approach, may this be about how to advance a novel research idea or how to change a university's operating model. Can we develop innovative approaches by consensus?

Most academic leaders promised during their interview for the role to be a change agent and to advance the organizations they want to lead. How do we live up to such promises when in recent times as some claim, progress has been stagnating? There are cultural reasons why we have seen less progress since 1970 in comparison to the century before during which the internal combustion engine, sanitation, synthetic fertilizer, antibiotics, vaccinations, nuclear power and modern air travel were invented. However, it's naïve to blame changes in culture for this stagnation as our past overly positive view on industrial progress has put us on a path toward the destruction of our environment, e.g., fossil fuel exploitation, deforestation, or the introduction of invasive species to control pests as demonstrated with the Cane Toad plague in Australia.

A more nuanced view is needed that embraces technological progress while ensuring that the global society can benefit while preventing harm. Claiming advances in computer and information technology, for example, the Internet and artificial intelligence, to showcase more recent progress forgets that we had similar advances pre-1970 with the advent of radio and television. (One might also quip that antibiotics were more beneficial to humanity than X (formerly Twitter).) An interview of Jason Crawford intrigued me by providing some ideas about what we, as academic leaders, can do to overcome some of the barriers to progress (Piper, 2021).

On the largest scale, we need to advance the message that technological progress is, overall, a good thing for humanity that has extended life expectancy and improved our well-being. Technology and the acceptance of science are the fundamental ingredients to this progress; thus, as academics, we need to fight against science denial and cuts in research and education funding. On a societal scale, political gridlock prevents progress as politicians think increasingly more about elections than about reforming broken regulatory systems or introducing evidence-based policies. A Grattan Institute Report analyzed this problem in the Australian context, and its findings are instructive as many observations and recommendations are transferable (Daley, 2021).

Back to the organizational scale that concerns us here. Centralization might stifle paradigm shifting innovation. Crawford argues that centralized decisions about research and development funding result in increased homogeneity in research that might "quash[] something that would be the next breakthrough because it doesn't fit the status quo." And this brings us to the leadership scale that's important for us, as most of us cannot change government policies. What can we do to balance inclusion and consultation while not hiding behind a committee decision when it comes to investment in innovation (Some answers for this can be found in the Lesson 2: "Cultivate Humility")?

Our role, as academic leaders, is to take risks and to make decisions. We need to consult and ensure all voices are being heard, but I agree with Crawford that relying entirely on consensus is not the recipe for progress. Centralization helps when you run finance and procurement in an organization, but central decisions on what research and development ideas to pursue is a questionable practice at best.

Collaboration

Change requires collaboration, not just with our own staff, but with stake-holders across different areas of the organization. But what does collaboration mean in today's context? How do we work creatively together to push our universities to the next level instead of just focusing on business as usual? Sending each other more e-mails is clearly not the way to go, and the introduction of Activity Based Working areas has not lived up to its promises and seems to be universally rejected by staff (Veldhoen Company, 2022).

If we want to trigger productive collaboration, the setting needs to follow function. In other words, deep-work requires solitude and immersion into one task. *Deep Work: Rules for Focused Success in a Distracted World* by Cal Newport suggests a strictly bimodal approach to work settings with a deep-work and a connected-life mode (Newport, 2016). I think this model for personal work can be applied to teams as well. You want to encourage your staff to spend quality time working on solutions, ideas, projects and so on. But these stretches of mostly solitary (or small team) work need to be augmented with meaningful and effective group work. Your role as leader is to establish ground rules that allow your staff (1) to work alone under the best conditions without disturbances and with proper resources to get the job done; and (2) to engage in purposeful interactions that encourage the exchange of ideas and collaboration in a psychological safe environment.

I believe that mixing the two modes is the root cause of low productivity and burnout in the modern office world. Working in a large space that permits serendipitous interactions and constant exposure to the projects other staff members are working on seems to be a typical ISLGIAT (It Seemed Like A Good Idea At The Time). However, Schwartz and Porath report that in a large survey "[o]nly 20 percent of respondents said they were able to focus on one task at a time at work, but those who could were 50 percent more engaged" (Schwartz & Porath, 2014). As leaders it is our duty of care to create an environment for our staff in which they can thrive and feel engaged.

David Brooks writes in *The Art of Focus*: "…look at the way children learn in groups. They make discoveries alone, but bring their treasures to the group. Then the group crowds around and hashes it out. In conversation, conflict, confusion and uncertainty can be metabolized and digested through somebody else. If the group sets a specific problem for itself, and then sets a tight deadline to come up with answers, the free digression of conversation will provide occasions in which people are surprised by their own minds" (Brooks,

2014). Let's bring our teams back to their productive childhood experiences to change how we run academic institutions.

Nurture an Agile Mind

As leaders we know that change is inevitable and that our teams will need to adjust to that change. For me, it is often surprising when I enter a new organization and find staff who believe that the status quo will last until they retire. The argument that "we have always done it this way" seems to resonate with many even though it makes no claim of rationality in my view. It is very easy to snap when you are confronted with claims such as that of the late Christopher Hitchens, "What else was to be expected of something that was produced by the close cousins of chimpanzees? Infallibility?" (Hitchens, 2007). However, we need to remember that all individuals have been formed by genes and their environment, things they can typically not influence. As the human body is 90% water, we are all basically just cucumbers with anxiety.

When you consider joining a new organization, you might want to check out its appetite for change, especially if you are specifically recruited to lead a major change program. Your internal warning signs should flash if you talk to members of this organization giving you the impression that "incremental politics have won over initiative and inertia has become a proven leader" (Prelinger, 2011). I have advised several of my mentees against taking on roles in organizations that are recalcitrant but try to fix their cultural problem by recruiting a single leader in one of the most resistant areas who is then supposed to turn things around in an environment that is not ready for change.

How can you tell if an organization is not conducive for change? In my observations, widespread attitudes against change in an organization can be determined by three easy to spot characteristics: First, if an organization is described as "generational," meaning several generations of one family make up the staff. Second, it is a reliable indication for problems if the tenure of senior leaders is longer than 10 years—a *Harvard Business Review* article describes how a long CEO tenure can hurt performance (Luo et al., 2013). And third and probably most important, large change comes rarely from an organization that is at the center of the system, as they tend to think linearly and have only a limited incentive to cause disruption because of the opportunity costs they might forgo. The latter characteristics were described with a fitting analogy by Vinod Khosla, founder of Sun Microsystems and who runs one of the most successful venture capital firms in the world: "Walmart didn't change retail; Amazon did, and it made it pretty damn uncomfortable for all other retailers. Boeing and Lockheed didn't change space; SpaceX did. General Motors and Volkswagen didn't change electric cars or self-driving cars; it was Waymo and Tesla. NBC and CBS didn't change media; it was Twitter, Facebook, and You-Tube. I am hard-pressed to find one large change that came from an institutional source in that area. If you do find one, tell me" (Khosla, 2018).

I have read the techniques suggested by Sarah Young, the founder and lead coach of Vision Insight, that prepare you for change (Young, 2017) and have adapted her text to fit into the framework of this book:

1. *Acceptance:* Take the time to acknowledge that the world is changing, will never stop changing and that the speed of change will only get quicker and quicker. You and your staff need to start learning to be okay with that and not fearful of it. Uncertainty needs to be balanced against the possibilities change brings. As leader find the people who are embracing change and surround yourself with them. Connect to the influencers and pull them to your side. While we need to engage in consultation and be open for critique, do not spend too much time with those who talk endlessly about how terrible change is and the negative effects of it. This is just adding oxygen to the fire.

2. *Mindfulness:* This is the art of bringing your attention and energy to the present moment, which is crucial for many leadership challenges, but especially to situations of change. More about this technique under Lesson 1 "Be Nice." Also note that during these complicated conversations that are always part of a change, for instance, when you explain to a staff member that he will be declared redundant, it is helpful to change your emotions to a kind attitude toward your conversation partner. This is hard, being angry is so much easier, but loving-kindness meditation will support you.

3. *Expanding your comfort zone:* The majority of us love our comfort zones. They are relaxing, non-confronting and a great place to hide. However, they can also be unfulfilling, boring, may cause us to be left behind or leave us with a feeling that something is missing in our lives. Explain to your staff that not much will grow in a comfort zone, so if they want to get to the next level, aspire to a promotion or a merit pay raise, change is a perfect opportunity to get there faster. Young suggests that expanding your comfort zone means doing things that make you feel slightly uncomfortable. For example, mixing up your daily routines, walking into a networking event where you know no-one, getting your coffee and lunch from a different cafe every day, taking a different route to work or visiting places that you have never been to before.

Tell Stories With Charisma

All of the aforementioned techniques sound depressing as it appears next to impossible to "bend people to your will" as a *The Atlantic* article by Matthew Hutson put it (Hutson, 2016). Clearly, you need to have some legitimacy when you lead an organization, like for me being the dean of a dental school, it goes without saying that I should be a dentist, so I am "part of the club." This does not mean I have to be the best dentist, or as in my case, I need to still practice, but if I want to talk to people, they need to know that you are coming from a position of understanding and general insight. However, while knowledge and expertise are preconditions, it is not sufficient to change people's minds. Hutson writes that people "want someone who can make a compelling pitch and inspire a sense of urgency—someone with charisma." Charisma is nothing divine or mysterious, but can be defined as the ability to convince followers that you can get other members of a wider group to cooperate, which in turn signals to your followers your ability to benefit the group by increasing the perceived likelihood that cooperation will bring success to the group (Grabo & van Vugt, 2016). This makes sense from an evolutionary standpoint, but how do we translate this into today's world?

I try to be a storyteller about the future, which is described as a "charismatic tactic" (Hutson, 2016). When I do this, I attempt to weave my audience into the story, so they see themselves in the proposed future. You also want to partner with other stakeholders, like in the HR area, who then tell the same story from their perspective to reinforce the message. As stated above, we are not going to learn from numbers by deducing the particular from the general, but rather likely to infer the general from the particular (Nisbett & Borgida, 1975). Kahneman writes ". . . even compelling causal statistics will not change long held beliefs or beliefs rooted in personal experience. On the other hand, surprising individual cases have a powerful impact and are a more effective tool for teaching" (Kahneman, 2013).

Getting to a shared vision in any relationship, community, or organization requires embracing conflict and thoughtfully resolving it—not shying away from it. Such conflict can occur on an individual level when you encounter CAVE people (CAVE = Citizens Against Virtually Everything) or on an institutional level if you clash with existing policies, rules, or just common practice. Russell Ackoff encapsulates the latter as "The level of conformity in an organization is in inverse proportion to its creative ability" (Ackoff et al., 2007).

What else signals charisma to your staff? Mental speed has been found as a stronger contributor to charisma, more than IQ or personality. That means you want to be able to give speedy answers to general-knowledge questions which makes you, in the eyes of your followers, quick-witted and funny. Von Hippel et al. write that mental speed "has the potential to play a role in social intelligence. For example, mental speed allows people to judge situational demands rapidly, consider a wide repertoire of responses within a socially appropriate response window, mask inappropriate initial reactions by rapidly presenting a nondominant response, and make time-sensitive humorous associations" (von Hippel et al., 2016).

Most important for us here is that charisma can be taught as shown by Antonakis et al. who trained middle managers and MBA students in CLT which stands for Charismatic Leadership Tactics (Antonakis et al., 2011):

Verbal Tactics
- Use metaphors as effective persuasion devices that affect information processing and framing by simplifying messaging and by stirring emotions as well as aiding recall.
- Use stories and anecdotes to make the message understandable and easy to remember.
- Demonstrate moral conviction and share the sentiment of the collective to be recognized as a representative of the group.
- Set high expectations for yourself and your followers and communicate confidence that these goals can be met.
- Use the following rhetorical devices: contrast (to frame and focus the message), lists (to give the impression of completeness), rhetorical questions (to create anticipation and puzzle that require and answer).

Nonverbal Tactics
- Convey your emotional state whether positive or negative to demonstrate passion and obtain support.
- Use body gestures and facial expressions.
- Use an animated voice tone to make the message memorable.

What I sometimes do, and I admit it is usually a painful and somewhat masochistic exercise, is to record myself when giving a speech or presentation for my own review purposes. It is amazing how often you can come up with ideas on how you could have expressed yourself better to improve your message.

Further Readings

Leadership on the Line: Staying Alive Through the Dangers of Change by Ronald Heifetz and Marty Linsky (R. A. Heifetz & Linsky, 2017). This classic on change leadership was written by Ronald Heifetz who is a cofounder of the international leadership and consulting practice Cambridge Leadership Associates (CLA) and the founding director of the Center for Public Leadership at the Harvard Kennedy School. The coauthor, Marty Linsky, is a cofounder of CLA and has taught at the Kennedy School for more than 25 years.

Change: How to Make Big Things Happen by Damon Centola (Centola, 2021). The book's central thesis is that you need to persuade people in the periphery instead of trying to influence the top influencer because the "social star" will not adopt the new behavior until a large growing number of their audience has adopted it. The social star is only one link in the chain of spreading social change. Centola argues that the "star" can be a roadblock to actual change if you put too much effort into persuading this person. Instead, you should use a more "wide bridges" approach to change.

"Level 5 Leadership: The Triumph of Humility and Fierce Resolve" by Jim Collins (Collins, 2005). This 2005 *Harvard Business Review* article will introduce you to Jim Collins, one of the great authors in the leadership and organizational theory space. Collins authored the best-selling business book *Good to Great: Why Some Companies Make the Leap…And Others Don't* (Collins, 2011) which are reflected in this article.

"How to speak so that people want to listen" by Julian Treasure (Treasure, 2013). Inspiring people with charisma is easier when you know how to give impactful speeches. I have struggled with this for a long time as learning Russian for 10 years in East Germany was not the ideal preparation for an academic career in the United States. Everyone can learn to become a better speaker. Julian Treasure, in his TED talk, demonstrates the how-to of powerful speaking—from some handy vocal exercises to tips on how to speak with empathy.

Change Theorists Wiki (R. A. Heifetz, 2007). This somewhat defunct wiki provides plenty of tables, overviews and excerpts from various leadership books that allow you to decide where to dive deeper and explore books and articles.

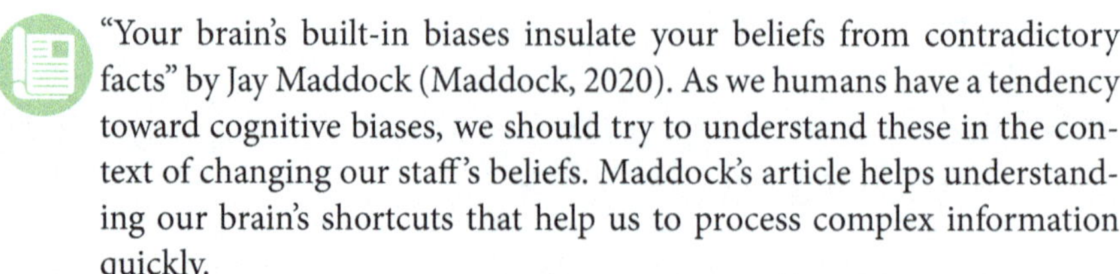

"Your brain's built-in biases insulate your beliefs from contradictory facts" by Jay Maddock (Maddock, 2020). As we humans have a tendency toward cognitive biases, we should try to understand these in the context of changing our staff's beliefs. Maddock's article helps understanding our brain's shortcuts that help us to process complex information quickly.

"Collaborative Overload" by Rob Cross, Reb Rebele and Adam Grant (Cross et al., 2016) argues that we suffer from collaborative overload as "time spent by managers and employees in collaborative activities has ballooned by 50% or more." The article's key message can be found in this paragraph: "Consider a typical week in your own organization. How much time do people spend in meetings, on the phone, and responding to e-mails? At many companies the proportion hovers around 80%, leaving employees little time for all the critical work they must complete on their own. Performance suffers as they are buried under an avalanche of requests for input or advice, access to resources, or attendance at a meeting. They take assignments home, and soon, according to a large body of evidence on stress, burnout and turnover become real risks."

"Good governance a steel rod in a crisis" by Mary Haines (Haines, 2020). Haines writes on LinkedIn about the value of good governance in times of crisis and change arguing that good people need to be supported by strong and resilient systems, founded on good governance. Effective governance includes "(1) setting, guiding and monitoring the future direction of the business (Strategy), (2) establishing appropriate control processes and accountability systems (Risk management), (3) ensuring that the business operates within its relevant legal boundaries (Compliance), (4) driving the performance of the business through the management team (Monitoring), (5) guiding the development of the business culture internally and externally (Cultural tone)."

"The real difficulty in changing any enterprise lies not in developing new ideas but in escaping from the old ones."
John Maynard Keynes, British economist (1883–1946)

Think and Work Strategically

"Strategy without tactics is the slowest route to victory.
Tactics without strategy is the noise before defeat."
Sun Tzu, Chinese general, military strategist, and philosopher, 6th century BC

As leaders we are supposed to work strategically and not operationally. But we also must be aware of the danger of prioritizing strategy over actions on the ground. If we exclusively act at a level that removes us from the action, we are likely to be judged as disconnected. We have all attended offsite strategic planning retreats that were filled with the excitement of developing a new mission statement to return on Monday to the office to find the same old routines, the painstakingly developed long-term goals quickly forgotten. The question is, how do we strike the right balance between leadership toward the greater goals and operational management of the daily issues?

Field Marshal Sir William Slim was governor general of Australia at the time he wrote in 1957: "Leadership is of the spirit, compounded of personality and vision; its practice is an art. Management is of the mind, more a matter of accurate calculation, of statistics, of methods, timetables, and routine; its practice is a science. Managers are necessary; leaders are essential" (Slim, 1957). If you do not know where you are going, you are unlikely to arrive; but if you know where you are going you cannot arrive there on your own.

Working strategically requires having allies in the leadership team that surrounds you. These can be superiors, peers, or your own team that you have assembled around you. In the past, it was common to consult with a team of domain experts during regular executive-level meetings, for instance, getting the latest updates on the financial situation of the organization during a brief and thoughtful interpretation of the numbers by the chief financial officer. You worked with colleagues together on problems too difficult for any single mind to solve. Now, problem solving looks different, as leaders often have access to dashboards displaying the latest management information in colorful charts, including the up-to-the-minute financial information. When you as leader sit, or stand if you have one of those fancy height adjustable standing desks, in front of your computer you have full access to all information, but how do you interpret them in the context of your team, in relation to the entire organization, in the context of the national or global economy?

For this, you will need a team of advisors who help you to translate data into information and then into knowledge that helps you to make decisions. But can you trust all of them to only have the organization's best interest in mind, or do they prioritize their own areas to benefit their teams over the goals of the larger organization? On this topic, my friend John Halamka borrows from Heifetz (R. Heifetz & Linsky, 2002) and writes in his blog "Assess your peers and your superiors frequently. Imagine yourself on a balcony watching the people in your organization as if you were watching a play. Understand the self-interest of each character. Just as personalities would be described in a work of fiction, you'll see the self-interested careerist, the servant leader, the manipulator, the fair weather friend, and the person you'd want in your foxhole during battle" (Halamka, 2015a). John knows what he is talking about when it comes to strategy and leadership as he is an Emergency Department doctor, Professor at Harvard and was CIO of a major Boston hospital before becoming president of the Mayo Clinic Platform.

But what about all the small things you are required to do, the things that make us often wonder if the work we are doing is at the top of our expertise, or if we just click checkmarks that mean little. We all tend to ignore essential activities when something unimportant is available that requires limited effort. Some might have heard about this as the Bikeshedding Effect, also known as the Law of Triviality, which describes our tendency to spend massive amounts of time on trivial matters (Parrish, 2020e). We often get bogged down so much with e-mail that we do not have enough time to devote to the important decisions. There are also opportunity costs, meaning that while we do trivial things, such as writing and reading e-mails, we are not able to engage in another activity. We essentially trade-off another activity with triviality.

Astro Teller, leader of X, the so-called moonshot factory at Alphabet, the parent company of Google, tells an "allegorical tale of a firm that has to get a monkey to stand on top of a 10 ft pedestal and recite passages from Shakespeare. Where would you begin? he asks. To show off early progress to bosses and investors, many people would start with the pedestal. That is the worst possible choice, Teller says. 'You can always build the pedestal. All of the risk and the learning comes from the extremely hard work of first training the monkey.' An X saying is '#MonkeyFirst'—yes, with the hashtag—and it means 'do the hardest thing first'" (Thompson, 2017).

Lastly, strategic thinking is important for your career development. The more senior you are, the more strategic you need to act. This sentence seems extremely obvious, but what we often forget is that most leaders worked many hours beyond the expected to get to their leadership position; however, once we have achieved our leadership position, we need different skills to succeed. In fact, Goldsmith argues in his book *What Got You Here Won't Get You There* (Goldsmith & Reiter, 2007) "that many of the behaviors that initially propel high-achievers up the corporate ladder are paradoxically the same ones preventing them from reaching the very top: habits such as winning too much (the need to win every workplace disagreement, even when it does not matter), adding too much value (adding your two cents to every discussion), and goal obsession (becoming so wrapped up in achieving short-term goals that you forget the larger mission). Early in your career, these behaviors demonstrate that you are driven. But the moment you step into a position of leadership, they become counterproductive" (R. Friedman, 2014). While writing this paragraph I was reminded of a comment made by Sir Eric Thomas, president of Bristol University, when he spoke here in Sydney a few years ago. He recounted the interview for his university president role during which he said, "You should hire me because I do not work on trains, but I daydream."

How can you be creative as a leader and come up with new ideas and strategies? Paul Graham, who is computer scientist, venture capitalist and essayist, says "There are some kinds of work that you cannot do well without thinking differently from your peers. To be a successful scientist, for example, it's not enough just to be correct. Your ideas must be both correct and novel. You can't publish papers saying things other people already know. You need to say things no one else has realized yet." He continues to explain that one way to achieve this is by "who[m] you surround yourself with. If you're surrounded by conventional-minded people, it will constrain which ideas you can express, and that in turn will constrain which ideas you have. But if you surround yourself with independent-minded people, you'll have the opposite experience:

hearing other people say surprising things will encourage you to, and to think of more" (Graham, 2020).

Synchronous or Asynchronous Collaboration

If we want to think and work strategically with our teams, we need to decide how we are going to do this in today's technologically enhanced and pandemic-shaped world of hybrid meetings and flexible work arrangements. Cal Newport writes that "for much of workplace history, collaboration among colleagues was synchronous by default," and while letter writing was introduced eventually, "it was too slow for day-to-day collaboration" (Newport, 2019). All pre-e-mail intra-office mail systems, e.g., pneumatic tubes for message cylinders, were costly and inefficient. Thus, to no one's surprise, "e-mail emerged as the killer app for bringing asynchronous communication to the office." I am sure that we can all confirm that, "with the arrival of practical asynchronous communication, people replaced a significant portion of the interaction that used to unfold in person with on-demand digital messaging, and they haven't looked back." While e-mail in itself is not a bad thing, "shifting away from synchronous interaction makes coordination more complex. The dream of replacing the quick phone call with an even quicker e-mail message didn't come to fruition; instead, what once could have been resolved in a few minutes on the phone now takes a dozen back-and-forth messages to sort out."

So, now we know why we are in today's e-mail mess; it is because the large experiment that attempted to prove the hypothesis that asynchrony in the office would increase productivity failed. What can we do about this? Turn off the e-mail servers? Hardly!

Newport offers a few examples of what leaders have tried to harness the power of collaboration to advance an organization strategically. Software developers often use a collaboration framework called Scrum. The basic idea is that the team meets once a day to talk about what they try to achieve for a particular project on this day and reflect on what they accomplished yesterday. Everyone learns what everyone is doing, sets priorities, and assigns tasks. "These meetings are often held standing up so that no one feels tempted to bloviate, and they typically last for around fifteen minutes. The idea that a quarter of an hour of structured synchrony is enough time to enable a full day of work might sound preposterous, but, for more than twelve million software developers, it seems to be working."

The other important idea that Newport shares was developed by a CEO who has replaced e-mail "with a 'regular rhythm' of meetings, which allows him to efficiently address issues in real-time. 'If you keep needing to send me urgent messages, then my assumption is that there's something broken about the way you're doing business,' he said." I am not sure if I am ready to try out either idea in my school right away. However, one of my goals is to move away from asynchronicity and provide more opportunities for staff members to interact and problem solve while interacting with each other.

Rational Strategic Decisions

Steven Pinker's book *Rationality: What It Is, Why It Seems Scarce, Why It Matters* brought rationality to the attention of academic leaders (Pinker, 2021). First, let's agree what we mean with rationality in this context. When you look up rationality at know-it-all Wikipedia, you will find that "Rationality is the quality or state of being rational—that is, being based on or agreeable to reason. Rationality implies the conformity of one's beliefs with one's reasons to believe, and of one's actions with one's reasons for action. 'Rationality' has different specialized meanings in philosophy, economics, sociology, psychology, evolutionary biology, game theory and political science."

Pinker provides common fallacies in our thinking as well as a large variety of tools that help us to improve the outcomes of our decision making. He is doing this by sharing a lot of hands-on examples that you can try out yourself—he provides many pictures and tables for the highly motivated reader. Pinker shares well-known and new research that helps us avoid these fallacies and which mental models (see Further Reading below, Farnam Street Knowledge Project) help us to make intelligent decisions.

But, as leaders we also need to be compassionate and take on responsibilities beyond the goals of the academic unit that we lead, for instance by considering the social and environmental impact of our decisions. Max Weber, the German scholar who proposed interpretations of social interactions that distinguished between four different idealized types of rationality (Kalberg, 1980), also acknowledged that emotions, value, and beliefs can guide decisions. Similarly, Pinker urges us to improve our thinking and to put it on more rational footing. But he then points out that not every rational decision is a right or just decision—something that resonated with me and reminded me of many decisions I had to make.

Recruit Change Agents

If you want to change your organization, you not only need a strategy, but people who can translate that strategic plan into results. Dean Stamoulis calls this Results Intelligence, a complement to Emotional Intelligence (Stamoulis, 2017). He argues that we need to balance both. "If someone is too focused on results, without paying attention to how they make people feel, morale will suffer. Conversely, if someone is too focused on emotions, without thinking about results, productivity will suffer." How do we find people who will get things done focusing on results while not driving their teams too hard? Stamoulis describes five characteristics of result-getters: (1) they have clear and precise end objectives seared into their minds, (2) they are single-minded about getting what they need to succeed, (3) they learn existing rules and processes, but then determine where they can skip steps to create efficiencies, (4) they are willing to face criticism for leaving out key people if doing so helps them advance their project more effectively, and (5) they are objective and clear-eyed in their evaluations about results, and failure is not an option. While I do not totally agree with Stamoulis's way of translating these characteristics into interview questions, I find them still refreshing compared to standard questions such as, "What attracted you to this position?" or hypothetical questions such as, "What would you do if faced with a tough deadline?" So here are interview questions suggested by Stamoulis:

"Where do you begin when developing an action plan to achieve a specific goal?

Good answer: Seeks to understand the big picture and desired end state, works backward from the end state to organize problems into logical buckets, is clear about which resources are needed, ensures the plans relate directly to the goal.

Poor answer: Overly general regarding magnitude of work, overly flexible and open ended, uncertain what good will look like, has trouble prioritizing tasks.

How do you keep track of initiatives in your area of responsibility?

Good answer: Has a strong project management mindset, clear organized plans, includes phases, timeframes and accountability. Checks on progress frequently.

Poor answer: Comfortable with a hodgepodge of actions and roles, allows plans to drift without regular review.

Is it acceptable to you to break rules or defy common industry practices? Why or why not?

Good answer: Respects rules but considers other ways to solve problems; believes rules can be a hindrance in some circumstances, uses gray areas to his or her advantage.

Poor answer: Always follows rules, too black and white in thinking, wants a clear rule book and consistently thinks about how things have been done in the past.

How do you decide which people to involve in a project or initiative?

Good answer: Has a strong orientation toward efficiency, is openly against bureaucracy and believes that consensus can lead to mediocrity. Believes in short and focused meetings, avoids and removes those viewed as roadblocks.

Poor answer: Overly inclusive, likes to think out loud with others, does not emphasize scope, overly concerned about offending others.

Tell me about a time when you were unsuccessful in reaching a goal.

Good answer: Will not let himself or herself fail, believes there is always a solution, has visible discomfort with not achieving objective.

Poor answer: Rationalizes, works too hard to justify a failure, blames others" (Stamoulis, 2017).

What have you tried to hide from your application and/or your LinkedIn profile?

Nobody likes to talk about failure and how to deal with things that do not work out as planned. And you will not find a lot about failures in resumes or learn about them during interviews except if you ask questions as suggested by Tyler Cowen in his book coauthored with Daniel Gross *Talent*, by asking unconventional questions, such as the one above or "What is a story one of your references might tell me when I call them?" (Cowen & Gross, 2022).

Practice Strategic Work

When I try to achieve strategic goals, I often use my computer and information science background. In the past, software development followed a paradigm of big-bang releases of products or updates. Some readers might remember when we heard news reports about Amazon or Google updating their shopping cart or their website's search functionality. Have you ever noticed that you have not heard about such updates in the last decade? The industry has abandoned "big project pipelines" that deliver after a long development process with a big product announcement at the end. Companies have recognized that, first, nothing ever goes smoothly with big releases which often result in media attention on the small bugs instead of the major new features. And second and more important, no one gets everything right in the first try. Thus, the new paradigm has shifted to continuously testing and iterating change in a manner more closely tuned to market changes and our environment (Ehrlich et al., 2017). For instance, most companies continuously change their websites for a small portion of their customers all the time, see how the changes are perceived, monitor how many users struggle, adjust accordingly, and then roll out the change gradually to a larger portion of their audience until everyone benefits from the innovation. The Institute for Healthcare Improvement uses a similar approach for quality improvement in healthcare settings, using the Plan Do Study Act (PDSA) cycle which helped develop the "Toyota way" of engaged, critical thinking employees and subsequent organizational success (Institute for Healthcare Improvement, 2020). I believe that incremental change acknowledges that with increasing age and professional advancement, at least my sense of epistemological modesty has been intensifying and with that I do not refer to political, scientific or religious matters, but to my understanding how little we can know about the effects of our decisions as the world around us is immeasurably complex (Brooks, 2015a). Even incremental success requires patience and celebration of the small victories, something that might be hard for those types of leaders who prefer big wins and big celebrations. However, in today's world that is not a winning strategy.

If we try many small projects, some of them maybe even competing against each other, in delivering a more significant effect then the other using different methodologies, by definition, many projects will fail. During an Institute of Medicine Roundtable on Value & Science-Driven Health Care, Thomas Graf, chief medical officer for population health and longitudinal care service lines at the Geisinger Health System said "What we want to do is fail forward fast. The concept is if you are not failing, you are not doing enough." He added that it is important to learn something from failure, to fail forward, and to keep iterating to the best design possible (Alper & Grossman, 2014).

The aforementioned conference-keynote pabulum "Fail fast! Fail often!" is not the way to go as in most organizations projects that don't work out are stigmatized, and their staff are reprimanded. Moreover, successful individuals are often not familiar with failure or how to get comfortable with it as pointed out by Chris Argyris (Argyris, 1991).

How can we as leaders achieve a culture in which it is permissible to fail without getting psychologically or career-wise damaged? Maybe we can learn from one of the most innovative companies, such as X? Derek Thompson writes in his exposé of Google's moonshot factory in *The Atlantic* that X's leaders had "to build a unique emotional climate, where people are excited to take big risks despite the inevitability of …'falling flat on their face.' X employees like to bring up the concept of 'psychological safety.' I initially winced when I heard the term, which sounded like New Age fluff. But it turns out to be an important element of X's culture … the company has also created financial rewards for team members who shut down projects that are likely to fail. … Some might consider these so-called failure bonuses to be a bad incentive. But … it's just smart business. The worst scenario for X is for many doomed projects to languish for years in purgatory, sucking up staff and resources. It is cheaper to reward employees who can say, 'We tried our best, and this just didn't work out." (Thompson, 2017). This is analogous to learning from near misses in the healthcare setting. Those are the best opportunities to understand how we can continuously improve patient safety (Barach, 2000).

Risk Assessment

There is no strategic decision without risk. Assessing risk, planning for contingencies and developing scenarios for the worst case and the best case are important tools to mitigate these risks. What role does your leadership team play in assessing risk? Thomas Zurbuchen, associate administrator at NASA Science Mission Directorate, answers: "For me, what I hate, if you want to tick me off, come show up and tell me everything is low risk. That makes me believe you haven't understood your job, right? Don't make me laugh, don't make me feel good. Make me feel scared and then make me feel comfortable because you're dealing with all the risks. Don't come and say it's all low risk. It is not low risk, it's rocket science" (Parrish, 2022c). Zurbuchen, interviewed by Shane Parrish, reflects about the transfer of worries from the team members to the leader. If the team is not worried then the leader needs to be worried about the inherent risks and that is, over time, stressful "and those worries pull them down so that the whole organization behaves in a way that they never bring a worry to you." Leaders feel more comfortable if they know that their people are worried about the risks, have thoroughly analyzed them and have drawn the appropriate conclusions to mitigate them.

So, the question for me is, how do we legitimize discussions about risks and the potential of failure? I often feel that we encourage, and even reward, project champions to emphasize the benefits of their proposed project. We want them to speak about the potential return on investment and how their initiative contributes to the strategy of the organization. Are champions of initiatives in your organization concerned about rejection when they talk about inherent risks and potential causes of failure of their proposal? Would you as leader be biased toward an initiative that is presented to you as risk free versus one whose champion has presented a list of potential risks of failure? Zurbuchen, who manages an $8 billion dollar research program at NASA, tells his teams "I need you to be worried more than me, then I'm feeling comfortable. I don't want you to be calm. I need you to be worried. That's what I want." For me, the conclusions of this risk conversation are that (1) I need to ensure that champions have thought about all the details of their proposal as well as about the risks. I need to make them feel comfortable to speak to me about these risks. If someone has no concerns, it should raise a red flag with me. And (2) that I clearly would not have the nerves to make quick go-no-go decisions for space rocket launches.

Incentives

Most universities lack the tools to pay financial bonuses or are not permitted to do so as they are governed by enterprise bargaining agreements with unions, but this doesn't prevent you as leader from praising your staff. My general observation is that we too often forget to call out success. Acknowledgement and praise are not only for children; people generally crave recognition and moral support. I have come to believe that a public display of appreciation motivates more than a confidential bonus payment. Another effective method of praise is to pass it along via your superior, who might not normally have visibility to the person you wish to acknowledge. I often send an e-mail to my boss with a short snippet about what was accomplished and ask her to e-mail the respective staff member or team adding words of her own but showing that she knows what happened. Invariably, I get feedback from staff saying that this "really made my day" or "I am so motivated to work towards our goal" in response. Some organizations have well developed electronic infrastructures to nominate a monthly "hero," send kudos at any time to a colleague, often with some mechanism for monthly or annual small but meaningful rewards for the awardees.

Deep Strategic Work

What can we do about the abovementioned Law of Triviality? First, we need to make a conscious effort to differentiate urgent from important. I am sure every reader can define the difference, but do we make a difference when we tackle urgent and important tasks?

We are all deadline-driven individuals and often perceive an unopened e-mail as a "deadline" to do something. Then, we start opening e-mails and begin to respond which always takes longer than expected. Many people feel at the end of the day that they have not accomplished much but are still exhausted. Zhu et al. describe the *Mere Urgency Effect* very well in their *Journal of Consumer Research* article: "Normatively speaking, people may choose to perform urgent tasks with short completion windows, instead of important tasks with larger outcomes, because important tasks are more difficult and further away from goal completion, urgent tasks involve more immediate and certain payoffs, or people want to finish the urgent tasks first and then work on important tasks later" (Zhu et al., 2018). So, try to spend less time on trivial tasks and prioritize important tasks even if this delays responding to e-mails and text messages. Create a window of time (perhaps twice daily) specifically for answering e-mail, but otherwise put your e-mails aside. If you do not have the luxury of a personal assistant to help you, see if it is possible to hire one from one of the sprawling virtual assistant companies, such as Invisible or Upwork. The pros and cons about this approach are well explained in a recent *The New Yorker* article by Nathan Heller (Heller, 2020).

Cal Newport, who writes about the intersection of digital technology and culture, claims that we are all working too shallow and accomplishing a lot that almost anyone, with a minimum of training, could do, such as writing e-mails or logistical planning. While this makes us feel productive, the work also feels empty and not really satisfying. In his book *So Good They Can't Ignore You* (Newport, 2012b) he suggested to shift to "deep work" by making it the centerpiece of your schedule which will generate three key benefits:

- Continuous improvement of the value of your work output.
- An increase in the total quantity of valuable output you produce.
- Deeper satisfaction (aka "passion") for your work.

Newport suggests a four-step process to get to deep work that is compelling and has worked for me personally—here partially quoted with some remarks from his blog (Newport, 2012a):

1. *Prepare:* Cultivate a ritual that transitions you from normal shallow work to the deep variety. This strategy works because it's easier to convince your mind to do the first step of a simple ritual than to dive straight into intense contemplation, for instance, you can shut the door, or get a cup of coffee, or as I do it personally, use the early morning hours when I am not disturbed.
2. *Clarify:* Deep work requires a clear image of the outcome you are seeking and a clear understanding of why it is valuable. Be specific about what success will look like and why that success is important. Finding the right questions is the hard part!
3. *Stretch:* Take your clear overall goal from the previous step and identify the next logical chunk of work. When you tackle this chunk, push for a result that is beyond—but not too far beyond—what's comfortable for your current skill level. This stretch is important to: (a) extract the most out of your current abilities; and (b) ensure that your abilities continue to improve.
4. *Obsess:* The nice thing about deep work is that it is a clear state of mind. You begin a session with a well-defined ritual, you work on a stretch chunk for 1–3 hours, then you finish and go rest. This clarity allows you to track how much time you spend in the state. This tracking gives you a number to try to improve.

If you want to shift your thinking from the trivial to the strategic, you will need to start *thinking*. I am fully aware that this sounds incredibly offensive to most readers who will claim that they think all the time. But what I am referring to here is not the *thinking* about technical matters or your problem-solving ability, but rather aim at the thinking in solitude described by William Deresiewicz in his 2010 essay "Solitude and Leadership—If you want others to follow, learn to be alone with your thoughts" (Deresiewicz, 2010): "Who can answer questions, but don't know how to ask them? Who can fulfill goals, but don't know how to set them? Who thinks about *how* to get things done, but not whether they're worth doing in the first place? What we have now are the greatest technocrats the world has ever seen, people who have been trained to be incredibly good at one specific thing, but who have no interest in anything beyond their area of expertise What we *don't* have are leaders."

And he continues: "What we don't have, in other words, are *thinkers*. People who can think for themselves." What is the opposite of thinking? Well, in my view it is multitasking as it "is not only not thinking, it impairs your ability to think. *Thinking means concentrating on one thing long enough to develop an idea about it*" (Deresiewicz, 2010). We know from research that switching between tasks increases cognitive load and therefore impedes our deeper thinking and generation of meaning. As cited in Nicholas Carr's book *The Shallows: What the Internet Is Doing to Our Brains* (N. Carr, 2010b), UCLA psychologist Russell Poldrack concludes from his research that "Switching between the two tasks short-circuited their understanding; they got the job done, but they lost its meaning. Our results suggest that learning facts and concepts will be worse if you learn them while you're distracted." While some authors defend distraction (Anderson, 2009), I would argue that if you want to create strategic direction for your organization as a leader, you want to create time for true thinking without distraction from e-mail and X (formerly Twitter). Clearly, searching the Web for a specific technical answer will yield a lot of information—as Anderson says, "The truly wise mind will harness, rather than abandon, the power of distraction"—but this is not part of thinking and working strategically! Author and comedian Andy Borowitz pointedly reminds us that "if Michelangelo had Twitter, the Sistine Chapel ceiling would still be white"—more on our tendency to get easily distracted can be found under Lesson 7: "Be Smart."

Prioritize Important Over Urgent

Alice Boyes provides some useful tips in her *Harvard Business Review* article (Boyes, 2018) on how to overcome the paradox that our most meaningful tasks are less likely to have deadlines than tasks that are relatively unimportant. I believe in implementing her strategies as I think they will incrementally move you in the right direction. I have adapted her advice to fit into the framework of this book and reduced most of her tips to short insights:

Schedule Important Tasks, and Give Yourself Way More Time Than You'll Need

This involves scheduling when and where you will tackle a certain important task. This means putting it on your calendar so that it blocks a block of time! This will make it dramatically more likely that the task will get done.

Isolate the Most Impactful Elements of Important Tasks

Breaking tasks into milestones or subgoals allows you to make incremental progress. If you set a lofty goal, you might end up never starting. Set a more realistic goal that brings you halfway there. If your task still feels intimidating, shrink it further until it feels doable. Then celebrate the success of reaching each milestone. Buy yourself some flowers or a nice latte!

Anticipate and Manage Feelings of Anxiety

Anticipating risks is important but thinking too much about things that could go wrong is anxiety-provoking. Working on important things typically requires having good skills for tolerating uncomfortable emotions. Acknowledging, labeling, and perhaps even visualizing the specific emotions that make an experience emotionally challenging is a basic but effective step for reducing those emotions.

Prioritize Tasks That Will Reduce Your Number of Urgent but Unimportant Tasks

There are ways to avoid the trap of being "too busy chasing cows to build a fence." If you encounter the same problems over and over you can outsource, automate, batch small tasks, eliminate tasks, streamline your workflow, or create templates for recurring tasks. Or invest some time once to set up a system that will save you time in the future. Here an outside set of eyes can be immensely helpful in finding a solution.

Further Readings

 "Google X and the Science of Radical Creativity" by Derek Thompson (Thompson, 2017). I have already mentioned this very interesting article about X, Alphabet's Moonshot factory, because it is so well positioned at the intersection of failure and innovation, but the entire article is very interesting from a leadership perspective.

 "Solitude and Leadership—If you want others to follow, learn to be alone with your thoughts" by William Deresiewicz (Deresiewicz, 2010). If you as leader really want to be known for being a strategic *think[er] on your own*, you might want to reflect on Deresiewicz writing: "Why is it so often that the best people are stuck in the middle and the people who are running things—the leaders—are the mediocrities? Because excellence isn't usually what gets you up the greasy pole. What gets you up is a talent for maneuvering. Kissing up to the people above you, kicking down to the people below you. Pleasing your teachers, pleasing your superiors, picking a powerful mentor and riding his coattails until it's time to stab him in the back. Jumping through hoops. … Leadership means finding a new direction, not simply putting yourself at the front of the herd that's heading toward the cliff."

 "Time Management: How to Focus on What's Important, Not Just What's Urgent" by Alice Boyes (Boyes, 2018). This *Harvard Business Review* article is extensively cited above, but I would encourage you to read the full version of Boyes' advice on how to get done with the important things in life—not all of them are about work.

 "Results Intelligence: Identifying People Who Get Things Done" by Dean Stamoulis (Stamoulis, 2017). I have already quoted the article by Dr Stamoulis, a managing director and leader of the Russell Reynolds Associates' Executive Assessment practice, extensively in this lesson, but there is more to find here, for instance, how the concept of Results Intelligence explains successes such as Tesla, SpaceX, or the invention of the light bulb. Dr. Stamoulis also authored the book *Senior Executive Assessment: A Key to Responsible Corporate Governance* (Stamoulis, 2015).

 "Why We Focus on Trivial Things: The Bikeshed Effect" by Shane Parrish (Parrish, 2020e). If you have never heard about the Bikeshed Effect or the Law of Triviality, I strongly recommend reading this very short article on Farnam Street which explains this metaphor illustrating our

strange tendency to spend excessive time on trivial matters, often glossing over important ones.

 "Mental Models: The Best Way to Make Intelligent Decisions (109 Models Explained)" by Shane Parrish (Parrish, 2019). Throughout this book, I often quote Parrish's posts on Farnam Street—this is not by accident as he is one of the smartest thinkers in my view. The mental models blog post provides tools to better understand the world. "Mental models are how we simplify complexity, why we consider some things more relevant than others, and how we reason. … The quality of our thinking is proportional to the models in our head and their usefulness in the situation at hand. The more models you have—the bigger your toolbox—the more likely you are to have the right models to see reality."

 "How to Manage the Strategic-Planning Process" by David D. Perlmutter (Perlmutter, 2019b). Perlmutter is a professor and dean of the College of Media & Communication at Texas Tech University. His book on promotion and tenure published by Harvard University Press, might be of interest to academic readers. Note that this article requires access to *The Chronicle*.

> *"It is not enough to do your best; you must know what to do,*
> *and then do your best."*
> W. Edwards Deming (1900–1993), pioneer of systems thinking

7

Be Smart

"The capacity of the human mind for formulating and solving complex problems is very small compared with the size of the problems whose solution is required for objectively rational behavior in the real world—or even for a reasonable approximation to such objective reality."
Herbert A. Simon (1916–2001), American economist,
political scientist, and cognitive psychologist

After the somewhat depressing opening quote by the Nobel Prize in Economics winner Herbert A. Simon, we need to acknowledge that everyone wants to be smart, or at least wants to appear smart. What does this mean for leadership and management? We have a Cambrian explosion of new technologies all around us, not just in the workplace but also at home, noting that the lines between work and home are blurring, especially in post-pandemic times.

We need to upend long-standing theories of managerial cognition: "no longer to make decisions under conditions of information scarcity; increasingly, it is to make decisions under conditions of information overload" (van Knippenberg et al., 2015). So, what is the problem? If we have enough information, then we can make decisions based on the facts and data. First, I think that it is increasingly impossible for leaders to efficiently deal with the combinatorial explosion that encompasses all the facts embedded in the myriad of spreadsheets, dashboards, papers, news, websites, etc. that come to our desks without the aid of information processing tools. Second, while we have no more information scarcity, but instead an overload of information, I am somewhat doubtful that we have more information available that actually matters.

The problem with an abundance of information, useful or not, is that too much information competes for the attention of individuals, groups, and organizations. This extra information acts as a distraction from the important information or from getting on with your work. Van Knippenberg et al. writes "The amount of information scales faster than the attention of human decision makers who have to make decisions about which information has priority, and what will be shunted away" (van Knippenberg et al., 2015).

In addition, we as humans must deal with the distraction problem, something that can be explained from an evolutionary perspective. Our tendency to be easily distracted can be attributed to our information processing capacity which requires information as input—as animals are foraging for food, we are foraging for information. Adam Gazzaley and Larry Rosen use this analogy in their book *The Distracted Mind: Ancient Brains in a High-Tech World* describing why we so easily fall prey to pop-up notifications, text messages and click on links that are not part of the task at hand (Gazzaley & Rosen, 2016). Herbert A. Simon already observed in 1957 that we need to be aware that information consumes attention (Simon, 1957). Others argue that "there is no such thing as information overload, there's only a filter failure" (Russ, 2008). We need to address information overload by developing everyone's transactive memory—knowledge of who knows what—a skill nobody taught us at school. I think we are at an immature stage of understanding these skills and even further away from effectively teaching them to our children at school. It took us a long time to figure out how to use books, but it will take even longer to figure out how to augment our mental capabilities with technology. The classic science fiction book *Rainbows End*, by Hugo Award winning author Vernor Vinge, depicts children who receive extensive training on just how to search and filter information—it is time that our schools live up to this future (Vinge, 2007).

However, we should be careful when judging too harshly against distractions, as tuning your attentional filters is a complex task that requires continuous readjustments. What do I mean by that? If you are concentrated and more focused you get a lot done resulting in higher productivity due to having fewer switching costs. Or, in other words, you are good at keeping distractions out while having high attentional filters. For many, creativity embodies the opposite as you want to be open to unexpected leaps and connections embracing more parallel processing. Or, again in other words, you are looking for distractions having low attentional filters (Harris, 2019).

This leads us to the issue of information sharing. Old-style management was driven by the desire to keep information close and share only sparingly with others inside your own organization. Your boss would commonly only share with you what you needed to know to do the job at hand. As already expressed in Lesson 3: "Be Helpful," I try to help everyone who asks politely and never withhold anything—obviously excluding confidential personnel information, corporate secrets that fall under non-disclosure agreements (NDAs) and so on. This has resulted over years in a network of people who are all too happy to share with me in return and allow me to understand their different thought worlds. This is a "meta-issue" as I get to know how information is distributed across organizational groups. Now, I can consult with experts on all kinds of matters with quick turn-around time that allows me to be smarter, or at least look smarter by making better decisions. I am sure that some high-tech companies cannot operate like that for patent reasons, etc., but most institutions' processes are quite public anyhow.

Generally speaking, I find it exceedingly important to associate and network with people who think differently. To illustrate this a bit further, allow me to digress to my early formative years and how they have influenced me. I studied and then worked as an academic in the dental school at the Berlin Charité. At the end of the 19th century the Charité was on its way to become the most famous hospital in the world with Rudolf Virchow working there, the founder of the modern health care systems; Robert Koch, the discoverer of the tuberculosis bacillus; Emil von Behring, whose work contributed greatly to the healing of diphtheria; and Paul Ehrlich, who developed the first drug against syphilis. However, when I studied there at the end of the 20th century, during the East German regime, nobody discovered anything. At the time, I was certainly not encouraged to reflect on this, or worse articulate the lack of collaboration opportunities—nobody was allowed to travel to connect with other researchers or even attend conferences in the West. The lack of access to technology and high-end instrumentation was a barrier to academic progression. I believe that this political oppression can explain my compulsive devotion to collaboration, diversity and the employment of computer and information science to improve health outcomes through research. It is probably not by accident that I am still striving for communal successes in these areas, now on the third continent. Wherever I have worked, I have tried to counter any restrictions on collaboration and mobility across geographical and disciplinary boundaries. So, maybe I am a bit biased here, having seen the East German society collapse after we were all told to think alike (we probably never did, but only pretended we did—this was already good enough for the collapse). I strongly believe that best ideas are born when people from different domains interact and collaborate (see Lesson 3: "Be Helpful").

Reading

Another way to get smarter is to read more instead of watching TV. Charlie Munger, Warren Buffett's longtime business partner at Berkshire Hathaway, says, "The best thing a human being can do is to help another human being know more" (Parrish, 2020d). When asked about how to get smart, Warren Buffet says, "I just sit in my office and read all day." He estimates that he spends 80% of his working day reading and thinking. In his authorized biography The Snowball, Buffett told this story: "Charlie, as a very young lawyer, was probably getting $20 an hour. He thought to himself, 'Who's my most valuable client?' And he decided it was himself. So, he decided to sell himself an hour each day. He did it early in the morning, working on these construction projects and real estate deals. Everybody should do this, be the client, and then work for other people, too, and sell yourself an hour a day. It's important to think about the opportunity cost of this hour. On [the] one hand, you can check Twitter, read some online news, and reply to a few emails while pretending to finish the memo that is supposed to be the focus of your attention. On the other hand, you can dedicate the time to improving yourself. In the short term, you're better off with the dopamine-laced rush of email and Twitter while multitasking. In the long term, the investment in learning something new and improving yourself goes further" (Parrish, 2020d). How do we operationalize this? Maybe set yourself a few goals, such as reading a book for 30 minutes a day or try not to watch TV one day per week.

Technology

Technology and information access have rapidly improved, a change which is heralded as a positive development practically everywhere. But there is a flipside to this rapid progress. Edward O. Wilson, an American sociobiologist, said in 2009 during a debate at the Harvard Museum of Natural History in Cambridge: "The real problem of humanity is the following: we have Paleolithic emotions, medieval institutions, and godlike technology" (Watson & Wilson, 2009). A combination that appears to have created quite some trouble when we consider the effects of social media on the political landscape, the mental health of young people and the gradual demise of investigative journalism, to name just a few problems.

Ed Hess, Professor of Business Administration and Batten Executive-in-Residence at the Darden Graduate School of Business, writes in the *Harvard Busi-*

ness Review, "Many experts believe that human beings will still be needed to do the jobs that require higher-order critical, creative, and innovative thinking and the jobs that require high emotional engagement to meet the needs of other human beings. The challenge for many of us is that we do not excel at those skills because of our natural cognitive and emotional proclivities: We are confirmation-seeking thinkers and ego-affirmation-seeking defensive reasoners. We will need to overcome those proclivities in order to take our thinking, listening, relating, and collaborating skills to a much higher level" (Hess, 2017). Andrew Ng, the famous artificial intelligence (AI) researcher, has likened AI to electricity in that it will be as transformative for us as electricity was for our ancestors. His central thesis is that in the age of AI 'Being Smart' will mean something completely different (Hess, 2017). When I see that we force our students to memorize something that can be easily looked up or when we strip them of any technological help while performing an exam, I ask myself how this kind of learning and testing will translate into the 21st century. We need to learn to work with AI, like our ancestors learned to use the power of steam and later electricity. Critical thinking and team collaboration will be important, not how many biochemistry formulas you can cram into your brain for the sake of a few days of reliable recall.

There are numerous examples of how to use technology to be smarter, but let me share one that really helped me. Tiago Forte posted a blog "The Secret Power of 'Read It Later' Apps" (Forte, 2015c), which significantly changed my information diet. Forte's main argument is that "the ability to read is becoming a source of competitive advantage in the world."

Why is this an issue for academic leaders? They can all read—one would hope. But we all know the amount of distractions that we cope with every day. At the end of a long working day, I am often exhausted and have limited motivation to search for something meaningful to read that I can finish before calling it a day. I often catch myself browsing the news and clicking on some interesting sounding headlines just to experience one of two situations: (1) The article was not what was promised in the headline, and I felt like wasting my time after a few minutes of reading; or (2) the item was excellent, and I wished I could highlight and annotate some thoughts for later use, which is impossible to do on my iPad's browser. In either case, advertisements distracted my reading, and the formatting was less than optimal for consumption on a tablet.

What can we do about this? I have adopted the strict rule for myself to not read anything immediately when I discover it. Just to be clear, I am referring here not to e-mails or business documents that require my attention nor to books or very long reports, but instead to articles, papers, news items, announcements, newsletter issues, articles linked from X (formerly Twitter) that peak my interest, printed speeches, and so on that were either recommended to me, I discovered on social media, or popped up in my e-mail inbox as links or full-text articles. Forte explains various apps that you can use to save articles for later reading, but I lack the bandwidth to try out a new piece of subscription technology that requires a learning curve. Thus, I use Evernote, which is already part of my standard technology stack. So here is my process that changed my information intake:

I use minimal time, less than 30 seconds, to decide if something is worthwhile to potentially read—note that this is not a final decision to read something, but just a preliminary assessment. If the answer is yes, then I clip it to Evernote, which can be done with the Evernote Web Clipper (Web Clipper: Save Web Pages, Articles, and PDFs, 2021) with the push of one button on all my devices. I forward it to my custom Evernote e-mail if it is an e-mail (Save Emails into Evernote, 2020). Both intake routes result in the same outcome; the source is stored as a Note in my Evernote Notebook called "Read it Later" with the title of the Webpage or the e-mail subject as note title.

In the evening, during natural breaks when sitting somewhere waiting for the next event, in public transport or the like, I open my iPad and pick one of the notes from the Read It Later Notebook. I select one that suits my mood and attention ability, either a more news article style one, something new, or an item from the "should read but might be boring" kind. Three key advantages are immediately apparent when I start reading: (1) My initial enthusiasm about an information item is very often dramatically diminished during this now second look at the article. Such disappointment is not a problem as the Delete Note button is only one click away; (2) There are no ads in the clipped article, and the formatting is clean and consistent, permitting a much better reading experience; (3) I can highlight any sections, add my thoughts at the top of the article, and note with whom I should share it if I decide it is worth doing so. After reading the note, I move it to another Notebook to be stored or archived. Alternatively, I move the note to my Actions Notebook for processing in the next few days, for instance if a follow-up is required, such as sending it to a colleague. In summary, while requiring some discipline by not reading anything immediately, this process has improved my information consumption dramatically!

Recruiting Smart People

Whom shall we recruit for new positions given the challenges and disruptive forces described above that will come with the advent of AI and advanced robotics? Are certificates, degrees, and educational attainment all we need to focus on as leaders who are responsible to build effective teams? How do we find the person who is going to be energized by unknowns? The role education can play, and which role it cannot play, is well described by Buchanan et al. in their background paper for the UNESCO Futures of Education initiative (Buchanan et al., 2021). They argue that "the point of education is to provide access to knowledge and skills which are not typically gained in the course of everyday life." I agree with Buchanan that education should provide us with "things such as focus, grit, curiosity, influence, empathy, teamwork as well as cognitive abilities such as making and expressing meaning." They further state that education will equip people "to handle changing life courses and challenges arising from Artificial Intelligence (AI) and a world drowning in information." We as leaders are often responsible for recruitment of new talent and should therefore be aware of an excessive strive for the "identification of the latest type of skills, which usually turn out to be very similar to the skills identified in the previous round." Buchanan argues that it is more important to look at "attributes of interest (e.g., creativity, collaboration, problem-solving) [that] are best acquired in the process of developing competence in and between specific domains of either academic or vocational/professional knowledge. They cannot be mastered in the abstract." Thus, instead of hunting talent that possesses a specific narrow skill, or a specific certificate, we need to look for staff who have a "broad disciplinary understanding (a holistic and diverse education), conceptual competence." Such a recruitment goal acknowledges that "education is a necessary but not sufficient condition for developing new domains of expertise." This is also the central hypothesis of *Talent,* a book coauthored by Tyler Cowen and Daniel Gross. They achieve effective identification of talent not based on conventional interviews or IQ tests, but by asking unconventional questions, such as "How do you feel you are different from the people at your current company?" or "What are 10 words your partner would use to describe you?" or "What are doing for self-improvement?" (Cowen & Gross, 2022). See also Lesson 6: "Think and Work Strategically."

Trying to Be (or at Least, Appear) Smart

I try to apply the lessons learned from Health Information Technology where we often use the "five rights" which stand for bringing the right information to the right person in the right format through the right channel at the right time (Osheroff, 2009).

I do have the problem that I cannot remember everything. Well, who would have thought that? Already in 1986, during the pre-Internet era, an article in the Annals of Internal Medicine complains that "[o]ne of the most frustrating failings of the human mind is its Lilliputian capacity for storing and retrieving important but infrequently used information" (Haynes et al., 1986). Thus, I am increasingly trying to augment my brain with technological support tools. I know that sounds bad, but people have been fighting progress for a long time—Luddites are not an invention of the 19th century. Nicolas Carr shares in his Atlantic article "Is Google Making us Stupid" that "[i]n Plato's Phaedrus, Socrates bemoaned the development of writing. He feared that, as people came to rely on the written word as a substitute for the knowledge they used to carry inside their heads, they would, in the words of one of the dialogue's characters, 'cease to exercise their memory and become forgetful.' And because they would be able to 'receive a quantity of information without proper instruction,' they would 'be thought very knowledgeable when they are for the most part quite ignorant.'" (N. Carr, 2008). Each new invention triggered push back, when books emerged, when radio was invented and then later TV, and finally the Internet (N. Carr, 2010b).

I do not think that we should push back on technology, instead we should focus on the fundamental problem with all these technologies. Atul Gawande points out, "What ultimately makes the difference is how well people use technology. We have devoted disastrously little attention to fostering those abilities" (Gawande, 2011). For instance, during the COVID-19 pandemic, we all engaged in many (too many!) scheduled video conferences, but how often have we picked up our favorite conferencing system to discuss something ad hoc, mimicking what we would do if our team were all to sit in one office? I can barely recall more than a few instances. Why is this? We talk more often in an unscheduled manner with our team when physically in the office.

I strongly support what Norman says about mobile devices—they cannot just be used for straightforward person-to-person communication—they are instead "cognitive artefacts" (Norman, 1991). However, this means we need to know how to use technology. While we, counting myself here belonging to the group of people who have reached the lunchtime of life, assume that everyone younger is proficient at using information technology tools, this is actually not the case as many young people are sorely lacking the skills needed to retrieve, analyze, and communicate information available online (Guy & Lownes-Jackson, 2010). What we need to differentiate when assessing our own skills and the skill of our staff is information literacy instead of being blinded by digital comfort. "No matter how much has been claimed about digital natives, the reality is that 'digital comfort' is not to be equated with 'technology proficiency', and most certainly not with 'information fluency'"(Oblinger, 2008). The lack of information literacy is not only limited to finding information, nowadays often equated with Googling an issue followed by a cut-and-paste, but also extends to basic skills like how to manipulate spreadsheets or how to use advanced functions in word processing software. Lacking these basic skills can slow down your team and thus has to be recognized and addressed with dedicated training. Sometimes this will require you to perform some observing of your staff or asking questions such as, "How did you do xyz?" You will be astonished at what you will find out sometimes!

If we believe the futurist Ray Kurzweil, then "Technology is the continuation of evolution by other means and is itself an evolution process" (Kurzweil, 2000). If that is the case, then we need to adapt to it by embracing the opportunities that technological advances provide by learning how to use technology in the most effective and efficient way.

Capture Ideas

As leaders we often have good ideas, at least <u>we</u> think we have, but as we cannot act on most ideas right away, the question is what do we do with them? "Do you obsessively write every single one down, but never look at them again? Or do you let it pass, thinking 'Well it probably wasn't that good of an idea anyway'? Both these extremes characterize someone with low creative self-esteem—they don't put much stock in their own ideas, according to Tiago Forte who writes further "The real potential of a digital organizational system is to be a tool for capturing and systematically reminding you of past ideas, inspirations, insights, and connections. The heart of creativity and innovation is making spontaneous connections between seemingly unrelated things, and products such as Evernote can, when used correctly, serve as a cognitive exoskeleton, not only protecting us from the ravages of forgetfulness but also amplifying our blows as we take on creative challenges" (Forte, 2015a).

How do I deal with keeping organized using information technology? The things that I want to keep "in my head" are usually stored in Evernote using David Allen's systemic approach of *Getting Things Done* (GTD) (Allen, n.d.-b). Allen writes in his book, "If choosing to do work that just showed up instead of doing work you predefined is a conscious choice, based on your best call. That's playing the game the best way you can. Most people, however, have major improvements to make in how they clarify, manage, and renegotiate their total inventory of projects and actions. If you let yourself get caught up in the urgencies of the moment, without feeling comfortable about what you're *not* dealing with, the result is frustration and anxiety" (Allen, 2015). I have loosely adopted David's personal productivity methodology and implemented it in Evernote (Allen, n.d.-a).

David uses a five-step process as outlined on his website:

1. *Capture:* Collect what has your attention. Write, record, or gather any and everything that has your attention into a collection tool.
2. *Clarify:* Process what it means. Is it actionable? If so, decide the next action and project (if more than one action is required). If not, decide if it is trash, reference, or something to put on hold.
3. *Organize:* Put it where it belongs. Park reminders of your categorized content in appropriate places.
4. *Reflect:* Review frequently. Update and review all pertinent system contents to regain control and focus.
5. *Engage:* Simply do. Use your trusted system to make action decisions with confidence and clarity.

A word of caution when you implement something like GTD in your organization. You want to make sure that your vital staff members who are in unique roles store organizational information in locations that can be accessed in case of their departure. I admit that I am mixing personal and business information in Evernote—nothing confidential or for which an official record needs to be kept, but hundreds, if not thousands, of little cheat sheets that make my life easier in my role. I am by no means a genius, but I had accumulated some organizational knowledge during my 15 years at the University of Pittsburgh. Most of this transactional knowledge was in my personal data store, in Evernote. Pitt, at the time, had no infrastructure to extract this information from me and make it useful to my successor. But even if an organization has such an electronic data repository that encapsulates organizational knowledge, it is hard to ensure these remain valuable resources rather than expensive investments that are quickly ignored (Hansen & Haas, 2001). This is a fundamental problem in my view—one that cannot be easily addressed by creating a lot of procedure and policy documents as they too often only scratch the surface and substantial costs are associated with collecting, storing, and making the information findable using intelligent tagging systems. Thus, me leaving Pitt was a difficult transaction with respect to knowledge transfer. While my new organization uses OneNote as part of the enterprise Office 365 implementation, one still needs to ensure that Notebooks are set up under role-based accounts to retain them after the departure of an individual staff member. And of course, then the information needs to be referred to and used.

Filtering information is a big challenge for everyone as following a scientific journal or an industry update magazine is not sufficient nowadays. Instead of trying to "follow the literature," I often "employ" experts to point me to the most important papers and resources in each area. I am not asking them directly for advice, but instead follow a few trusted professionals on X (formerly Twitter) or read their blogs. Can anything of value be said in 140 characters or in a short blog? Maybe not, but I do not aim to learn new things from X, but instead see what others read or look at. If you pick the right people to follow, this can become an extremely effective filtering machine. In addition, you want to use classical research tools, such as search on PubMed or on *Harvard Business Review*.

Another way to deal with information imbalances, is the fact that leaders know less than their staff on most topics and has been described by Laura Tingle: "You cannot know any more as a leader. Therefore, your role as a leader has changed to becoming the one figuring out what the best way is to frame problems, what the most important questions are to be asked" (Tingle, 2018).

Don't Waste Your Life on E-mail

Most people must deal with e-mail during a significant portion of their workday. Thus, I have decided to include an entire section specifically about e-mail here as every leader, in fact I would say, *every* person needs tackle this problem if she wants to be successful and act smart in the workplace. Addressing "the e-mail problem" is partially self-preservation as my grey hair is not a fashion statement—I just have received too many e-mails in my life. Because I am somewhat of a geek, I have always been able to transfer all my e-mails since early in my career, in the Jurassic period.

First, I will try to analyze the problem of e-mail communication and increase awareness about the complexity of the problem. After you are feeling miserable, I will offer some solutions, but please do not expect a panacea. I will try to canvas the main options for how we can curb the productivity drain by e-mail. I would caution against catastrophizing—as Stephen Pinker says in his book *Enlightening Now* "remember your history: the fact that something is bad today does not mean it was better in the past" (Pinker, 2018). We always had people who wrote too many letters or dictated too many memos—nothing new here, just faster.

Problems with E-mail: There are many problems with e-mail, but in my view, the root issue is related to the concept introduced by the economist and ecologist Garrett Hardin, called the "Tragedy of the Commons" (Hardin, 1968). Hardin states that in a system where a common resource is shared, with no individual responsible for the well-being of the resource, it tends to be depleted over time. E-mail is essentially free, but the resource it depletes is our attention. Observing the ever-increasing volume of e-mail, an end state of total depletion of our attention by e-mail doesn't seem to be too far-fetched.

Many of us have seen the online disinhibition effect, also known as *The Cyber Effect* as explained by Mary Aiken in her book of the same title (Aiken, 2016). A surprisingly large proportion of people write things on e-mail that we are certain they would have never uttered out loud in front of the person with whom they disagree. E-mail has undermined our standard for civility and eroded altruism.

E-mail also fuels the human tendency to want to do or say something. We all want to act even when our actions are not needed. On e-mail, you find people who offer solutions or input even when they do not know how to solve the problem. I have seen countless examples of this during the COVID-19 pandemic—suddenly everyone became an infectious disease expert—fortunately, none of my e-mail partners suggested barbecuing 5G towers to fight the spread of the virus (Donnelly, 2020).

Reply to All: This seems to be the most hated, and most used, feature in e-mail. While it is related to the previously mentioned desire to act, it has a different element. I believe that it reflects our upbringing which included greeting people whom we know—I am sure your mother taught you this when you were little. If someone says "hi" to us in the hallway in front of our office, we respond. Not responding would be perceived as extremely rude. So, our thinking goes that if our e-mail partner says "Hi" or "Dear" at the beginning of an e-mail or ends with "Have a good day" or even just "Thank you," we need to respond. To stand up in the eyes of our mothers, we need to demonstrate that we properly greet people back—what better way to show up our good upbringing by clicking "Reply to All"?

Our unnatural dependence on e-mail has surprised me many times. I once was working in a dental school that managed its own e-mail server. When the server was down for a few days due to a technical problem, many department chairs later commented that the outrage among their staff was probably worse than if a pay cut had been announced. This could reflect the fact that many staff members nowadays expect that they can use work e-mail for private purposes, or that they genuinely need e-mail to connect to collaborators and partners outside the institutions. However, the fervor due to the loss of e-mail functionality still astonishes me when compared with an electronic health record outage that plagued the same dental school for over three weeks.

Solutions: First, we need to acknowledge that we can't influence what we are sent from the outside. There is nothing we can do except for investing in Information and Communication Technology (ICT) solutions, such as installing proper spam filters and anti-phishing measures to prevent malicious e-mails penetrating our institutional systems. Thus, I will address how we can do something about the tsunami of e-mails from inside our own institutions. I will also stay away from most technical solutions, such as new e-mail features such as Focused Inbox for Outlook or Gmail's Customized Inbox as these give me anxiety because I have found they work only 95% of the time. I will not elaborate on how to address the multiple inbox problem that occurs when you do not forward your notifications to your e-mail inbox from O365 Teams, OneNote, Slack, or Canvas.

I have described in Lesson 2: "Cultivate Humility" how important listening is for us as leaders. We know that it is hard work to actively listen and show that we have understood what was conveyed to us by summarizing what was said. Now, let us translate this skill to e-mail communication! While there is often a long thread below our message that includes all the background information that one can wish for, most people do not have the time to wade through multiple pages of previous e-mails to explore the history of the issue or hunt for contextual clues. If it is important, employ the active listening technique of summarizing the issues at the top of the e-mail, the context and what you want to bring across.

How long should an e-mail be? Marketing research has shown that the ideal length of an e-mail is between 50 and 125 words (Renahan, 2018). I know that you think that your e-mails are certainly not in the "marketing" category, and are certainly not spam, but aren't you often trying to sell an idea or suggestion to your boss or staff? Long posts have triggered tl;dr (Too Long Didn't Read), now widely used on Reddit where authors place a shortened version of the story at the bottom for the people who do not want to read everything (Reddit, 2020).

I often ask myself how we survived prior to the arrival of e-mail. Clearly, we had memos and letters on paper, but if today's volume of e-mail had been put on paper, we would have run out of trees a long time ago. Now, we have an avalanche of e-mails, and we need to ask ourselves what matters—when we pull the camera back and see the big picture, we need to ask ourselves, is most of what we receive really needed? I suggest submitting e-mails of suspiciously low value to the already mentioned Alien Abduction test. This time we ask: if aliens come and remove this e-mail thread, what will not work anymore? If regular work life and the pursuit of our strategic goals go on like before, then it is not essential.

Never, ever use e-mail for conflict resolution! It is the wrong communication channel. The reasons for this are best explained by Kruger et al. in their article titled "Egocentrism over e-mail: Can we communicate as well as we think?" People only ascertain the intended tone on an e-mail message about 56% of the time, not much better than chance (Kruger et al., 2005). The research also found that people think they have correctly interpreted the tone 90% of the time. I hope that these numbers will once and for all stop our attempts to bring a certain tone across in an e-mail. It just does not work!

How do you feel when you get an e-mail that offends you? Our natural inclination, trained through hundreds of thousands of years in the African Savanna, is to fight back quickly before getting eaten. This natural reflex helped us survive back then but is not helpful anymore. Instead, we should use Hanlon's Razor as a tool (Parrish, 2020a). In short, we should only assume malice in an e-mail when the issue cannot be explained by error or plain stupidity. Shane Parrish explains "By not generally assuming that bad results are the fault of a bad actor, we look for options instead of missing opportunities. This model reminds us that people do make mistakes. It demands that we ask if there is another reasonable explanation for the events that have occurred. The explanation most likely to be right is the one that contains the least amount of intent." To help you accept that the offending e-mail was not intended to be so, consider that all humans suffer from attribution bias. When someone else does something poorly, such as write a seemingly angry e-mail, we blame the person's qualities—he's just rude. However, when someone else does something well, we give their situation credit—she can write well because she went to a private school. On the flip side, we only mess up when our situation is unlucky, and when we achieve something great it is all thanks to ourselves. It is possible, however, that your colleague simply had a bad day, or their cat sat on their keyboard and pressed send too soon.

There is only one way to write better: invest in becoming a good writer. Unclear writing is a sign of unclear thinking. Certainly, thousands of books on writing have been written. I looked at many in my quest to become a half-baked decent writer in a language that is not my native tongue and not the first foreign language I studied (I had to start with 10 years of intensive Russian in East Germany before I was allowed to study "the language of the enemy"). We need to spend time learning to compose better and more meaningful e-mails.

Use small tricks to reduce the e-mail volume for others, not only will they be thankful, but they will also try to reduce your e-mail burden—one would hope so. For instance, when you want to ask a group of individuals for their personal feedback, instead of putting them all into the CC which will result in people clicking Reply to All creating a deluge of messages, put the recipients into the BCC. You want to be transparent about such tricks and maybe start your message with "Hi Mary, John, Peter, Tina, and Jane (bcc-ed so I don't flood your inboxes with replies)."

The Future of E-mail: What will the future of e-communication look like? I predict that we will see a gradual improvement of our e-communication skills as we are just in the immature stage of understanding all this. It took us a long time to figure out how to use books, but it will take even longer to figure out how to augment our capabilities with technology.

I have adopted Chris Anderson and Jane Wulf's Email Charter which was stored at emailcharter.org, a now defunct link, so no reference for this one:

10 Rules to Reverse the E-mail Spiral

1. *Respect Recipients' Time:* This is the fundamental rule. As the message sender, the onus is on YOU to minimize the time your e-mail will take to process. Even if it means taking more time at your end before sending.
2. *Short or Slow Is Not Rude:* Let's mutually agree to cut each other some slack. Given the e-mail load we're all facing, it's OK if replies take a while coming and if they don't give detailed responses to all your questions. No one wants to come over as brusque, so please do not take it personally. We just want our lives back! Give yourself 48 hours to respond.

3. *Celebrate Clarity:* Start with a subject line that clearly labels the topic, and maybe includes a status category [Info], [Action], [Time Sens] [Low Priority]. Use crisp, muddle-free sentences. If the e-mail has to be longer than five sentences, make sure the first provides the basic reason for writing. Avoid strange fonts and colors. Longer thoughts might benefit from using an attached document.

4. *Quash Open-Ended Questions:* It is asking a lot to send someone an e-mail with four long paragraphs of turgid text followed by "Thoughts?." Even well-intended-but-open questions such as, "How can I help?" may not be that helpful. E-mail generosity requires simplifying, easy-to-answer questions. "Can I help best by a) calling, b) visiting, or c) staying right out of it?!" Remember, most people are not eager to work as your unpaid consultants.

5. *Slash Surplus cc's:* cc's are like mating bunnies. For every recipient you add, you are dramatically multiplying total response time. Not to be done lightly! When there are multiple recipients, please don't default to "Reply All." Maybe you only need to cc a couple of people on the original thread. Or none. Many people do not respond to e-mails in which they are listed in the cc field.

6. *Tighten the Thread:* Some e-mails depend on their meaning and context. Which means it's usually right to include the thread being responded to. But it's rare that a thread should extend to more than three e-mails. Before sending, cut what's not relevant. Or consider making a phone call instead.

7. *Attack Attachments:* Don't use graphics files as logos or signatures that appear as attachments. Time is wasted trying to see if there's something to open. Even worse is sending text as an attachment when it could have been included in the body of the e-mail.

8. *Give these Gifts:* EOM NNTR: If your e-mail message can be expressed in half a dozen words, just put it in the subject line, followed by EOM (= End of Message). This saves the recipient having to actually open the message. Ending a note with "No need to respond" or NNTR, is a wonderful act of generosity. Many acronyms confuse as much as help, but these two are golden and deserve wide adoption.

9. *Cut Contentless Responses:* You don't need to reply to every e-mail, especially not those that are themselves clear responses. An e-mail saying "Thanks for your note. I'm in." does not need you to reply "Great." That just cost someone another 30 seconds.

10. *Disconnect!* If we all agreed to spend less time doing e-mail, we'd all get less e-mail! Consider calendaring half-days at work where you can't go online. Or a commitment to e-mail-free weekends. Or an "auto-response" that references this charter. And don't forget to smell the roses.

"Is Google Making Us Stupid? What the Internet is doing to our brains" by Nicholas Carr (N. Carr, 2008). This Atlantic article concisely brings Nicholas' arguments against the Internet forward which can be summarized in this quote about our information consumption, "My mind now expects to take in information the way the Net distributes it: in a swiftly moving stream of particles. Once I was a scuba diver in the sea of words. Now I zip along the surface like a guy on a Jet Ski."

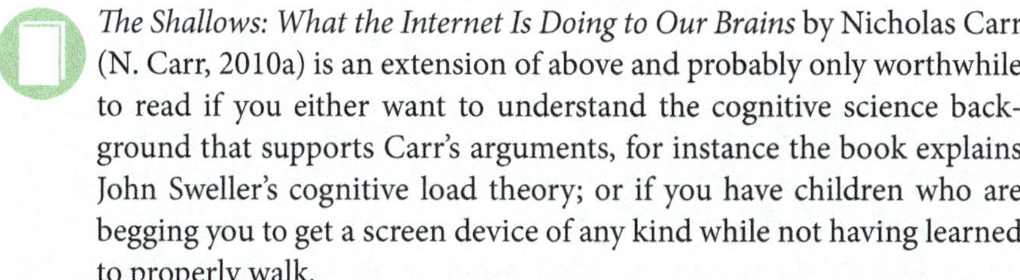

The Shallows: What the Internet Is Doing to Our Brains by Nicholas Carr (N. Carr, 2010a) is an extension of above and probably only worthwhile to read if you either want to understand the cognitive science background that supports Carr's arguments, for instance the book explains John Sweller's cognitive load theory; or if you have children who are begging you to get a screen device of any kind while not having learned to properly walk.

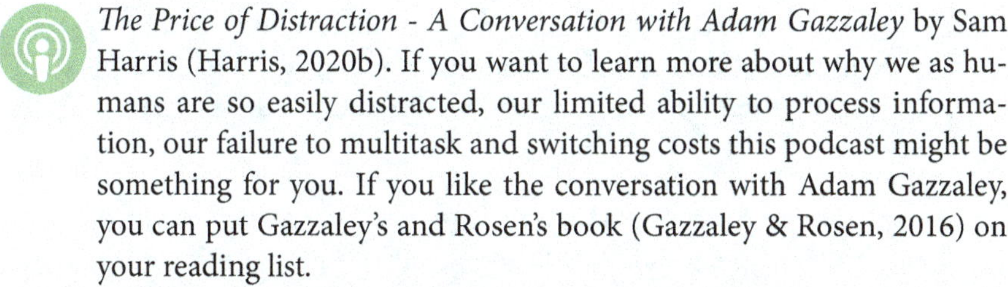

The Price of Distraction - A Conversation with Adam Gazzaley by Sam Harris (Harris, 2020b). If you want to learn more about why we as humans are so easily distracted, our limited ability to process information, our failure to multitask and switching costs this podcast might be something for you. If you like the conversation with Adam Gazzaley, you can put Gazzaley's and Rosen's book (Gazzaley & Rosen, 2016) on your reading list.

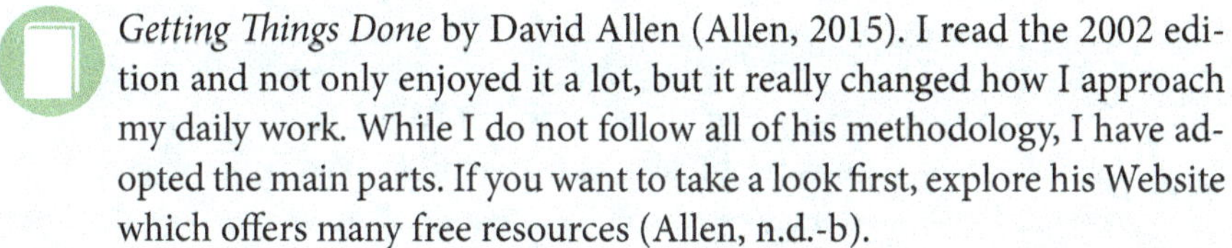

Getting Things Done by David Allen (Allen, 2015). I read the 2002 edition and not only enjoyed it a lot, but it really changed how I approach my daily work. While I do not follow all of his methodology, I have adopted the main parts. If you want to take a look first, explore his Website which offers many free resources (Allen, n.d.-b).

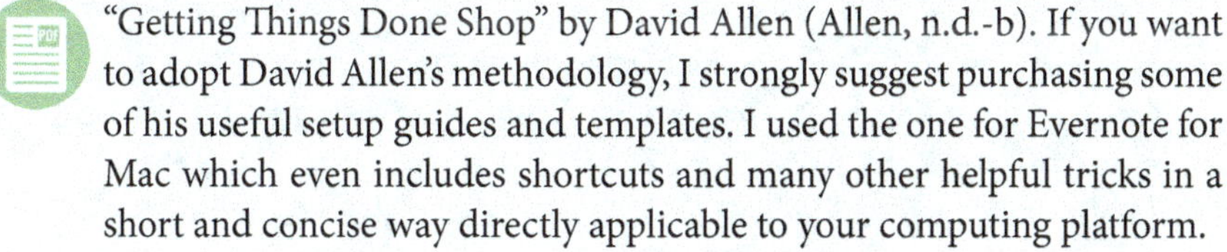

"Getting Things Done Shop" by David Allen (Allen, n.d.-b). If you want to adopt David Allen's methodology, I strongly suggest purchasing some of his useful setup guides and templates. I used the one for Evernote for Mac which even includes shortcuts and many other helpful tricks in a short and concise way directly applicable to your computing platform.

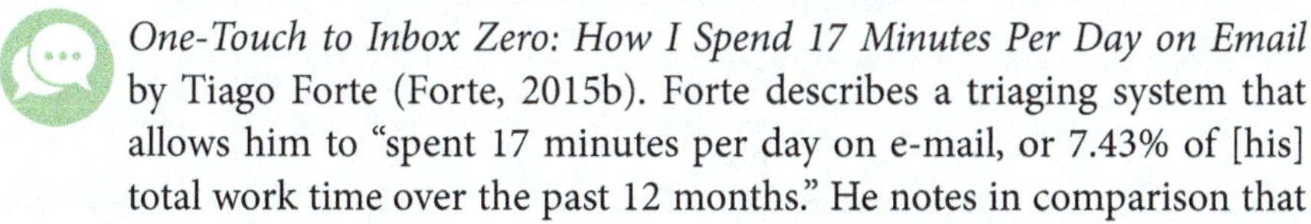

One-Touch to Inbox Zero: How I Spend 17 Minutes Per Day on Email by Tiago Forte (Forte, 2015b). Forte describes a triaging system that allows him to "spent 17 minutes per day on e-mail, or 7.43% of [his] total work time over the past 12 months." He notes in comparison that

"The average information worker, in contrast, spends 28% of their time reading, writing, and responding to e-mail—nearly 4 times as much." I completely agree with his overarching message that e-mail is for new input should not be used as a task list, calendar, or reminder system.

Evernote and the Brain: Designing Creativity Workflows by Tiago Forte (Forte, 2015a). This 7,000-word blog post goes beyond the technical explanations of how to organize your digital life by delving into the levers that we can use to promote creative thinking by creating a suitable cognitive environment—just storing is not good enough. While Forte is clearly promoting Evernote, everything he says can be used with other note taking programs.

21 Lessons for the 21st Century by Yuval Noah (Harari, 2018). I think this is a must-read book for all of us as we all need to explore how our minds will need to adapt to the second machine age. The book also explores questions of diversity, tolerance and cultural relativism that challenges our common notions about why diversity is so important in organizations and why it is dangerous to label cultures, companies and individuals as "intolerant" without asking who is intolerant of whom, or what? I also highly recommend reading other books by Yuval Noah Harari.

The Sense of Style: The Thinking Person's Guide to Writing in the 21st Century by Steven Pinker. This book really stands out in my view when it comes to better writing. The book is oriented toward our modern-day writing and use of syntax.

Style Lessons in Clarity and Grace by Joseph Williams (Williams, 2013). I would call this book the bible on clear writing as Williams explains like no one else how to make prose clear, flowing, logically organized while retaining elegance and beauty.

"Ask your staff 'What is the scariest thing I could ask you to do?'
Then, allow people to stretch by you asking them to do it."
Professor Robyn Ward AM FAHMS, Executive Dean and Pro
Vice-Chancellor Medicine and Health, Faculty of Medicine and
Health at The University of Sydney

8
Sleep Well

"The best bridge between despair and hope is a good night's sleep."
E. J. Cossman

I kept this one for last so you can go to sleep after reading this lesson. I also must admit that while we are all on a journey toward better leadership skills—when it comes to sleeping well, I have just started my journey. I have been known for only sleeping five to six hours each night, often being up at three or four in the morning working when no one disturbs me. This has been self-chosen and has not been forced upon me, although since I have moved to Australia, it became a necessity on some days when collaborating with researchers in the United States as it is the best time for mutually agreeable conference calls. So, I am certainly not a shining example of doing the right thing. But this does not mean that I don't understand the value of sleep.

Today's connectivity creates the expectation that you are always available. As an academic leader you often must work on weekends or deal with a student crisis, pandemic impact on teaching, a health issue of one of your academics or responding to unfavorable media coverage of your area of responsibility—none of these can wait until Monday morning. There is no reasonable excuse claiming that resolving such issues can wait and that your after-hours time is more important than the well-being of your students and staff or the reputation of your university. If you perceive such interruptions as stressful, you might have to think twice before taking on a senior leadership position in an university. On the other hand, if you love to solve problems, deal with the unexpected or just enjoy your work because the goals of your organization align with your personal goals, then this extra work should be something you thrive on.

There is also the perception that sleeping well conflicts with working hard. The opposite is actually the case. Spending more time on a task does not necessarily translate into better quality, for instance, we know that longer e-mails are less likely to be read (see Lesson 7: "Be Smart," Section about Email). Cody Delistraty writes about "how toiling away for more hours diminishes productivity. Why do so many do it anyway? It seems silly that many work long hours simply for the sake of having worked long hours. Perhaps the reason people overwork even when it is not for 'reward, punishment, or obligation' is because it holds great social cachet. Busyness implies hard work, which implies good character, a strong education, and either present or future affluence. The phrase, 'I can't; I'm busy,' sends a signal that you're not just an homme sérieux, but an important one at that" (Delistraty, 2014). Or, as one of my, here to remain unnamed, friends used to say, "If you can't make it with your brain, you can't make it with hours." Sleeping less and spending more time at work will not reap in the rewards one would expect!

Ron Friedman writes in *Harvard Business Review* about our decline in cognitive performance when we work too many hours with too little time left for sleep. "What happens to our interpersonal skills when we work ourselves to exhaustion? Studies indicate that when we're low on energy, we tend to misread those around us (Van Der Helm et al., 2010), typically in a more negative fashion. Happy faces appear more neutral. Neutral faces start to look like frowns. What's more, when we're fatigued we find it harder to resist lashing out at perceived slights (Gordon & Chen, 2014). Not only do we incorrectly perceive the world around us with more negativity, we're also more likely to act upon that information" (R. Friedman, 2014).

It is not a new finding that super hard work will reduce performance and the quality of your work; Plummer and Wilson remind us that "Henry Ford's primary motivation for cutting weekly hours from 48 to 40 was to reduce the number of errors his employees were making (Delistraty, 2014). Employers in several manufacturing industries have similarly found that they could maintain output and quality while decreasing employees' hours. If that weren't enough, according to research done at top strategy consulting firms, managers struggle to distinguish between those who work 80-hour weeks and those who work 50-60-hour weeks, suggesting that the extra work generally isn't noticed (Raid, 2015)" (Plummer & Wilson, 2018).

Regardless of whether you perceive evening or weekend interruptions as stress or as a welcome challenge, you still need to take care of the needs of your brain. Some of the facts presented in Matthew Walker's book "Why We Sleep" (Walker, 2017) are rather convincing, even I have to admit that. And I should point out that Walker is not a sensational science journalist but a professor of Neuroscience and Psychology at UC Berkeley, the Director of its Sleep and Neuroimaging Lab, and a former Professor of Psychiatry at Harvard University. He knows what he is talking about!

Let me share just two nuggets from his, for me personally, influential book. With the EU harmonization, Greece was forced to abandon siestas—shops stayed open, and work continued during the lunch hours. Even after controlling for all other factors, their population experienced a 37% increase in cardiovascular diseases. This finding seems to support that sleep is not just important for the brain but that sleep deprivation has an impact on general well-being. The second nugget is about researchers performing an experiment assessing college students' ability to learn: one group was permitted a proper night sleep while the other group pulled an all-nighter. Not going into all the details of the study setup that are well explained in Walker's book, after two full nights of recovery sleep, the effectiveness of learning between the two groups showed a 40% deficit in the ability of the sleep-deprived group to cram new facts into their brains. Conclusion: Never ever pull an "all-nighter"!

Go to Bed

But not now, you are supposed to finish this book first! What can we do about the need for proper sleep? It sounds easy to go to bed, and I am sure most of you in a leadership position will think that you will follow this advice after your retirement or when you have lost your job. But given the demands of your role, you feel disempowered to improve the current situation. Thus, the subheading "Go to Bed" will remain, for most of us, more aspirational. However, I want to present a few practical tips that can help us on our journey toward better sleep and to extend improved health and well-being. Something that we not only owe to our teams, but to our families and loved ones.

In my current role, I try to purposefully encourage my staff to take care of their health which includes sleep. It is, in my view, a Work Health Safety matter, even if they are supposed to sleep at home and not at work! For instance, I acknowledge that there are Morning Larks and Night Owls. This dichotomy has evolutionary reasons as the existence of these two types of sleepers has increased our survival chances by having alert individuals around in the early morning hours as well as late at night for detecting threats and defending the pack. Thus, allow yourself and others to follow their genetically determined pattern. Behavioral geneticist Robert Plomin has shown in his research that bending one's disposition is doomed because our behavioral traits are 50% inherited (Plomin, 2018). One of my best staff members is practically useless before 9 am. Thus, I will not schedule a meeting where this staff member is required before that time—why would I do otherwise if I want to maximize the output of my team and assure the well-being of my staff?

The decimation of sleep throughout industrialized nations has had a cat-astrophic impact on our health, argues Walker in his book. As leaders, we should try to reverse this trend in the interest of our staff and communities. One method that is easy to operationalize is to schedule e-mails to be sent during work hours. It is your personal choice as leader to work during week-ends or late at night, but this does not mean your staff should be forced to respond to you during these hours. Most readers, I am sure, will now argue that they do not expect their staff to respond, some of you might even make it a habit to explicitly state in the e-mail that they do not expect a response. Well, I think this approach is a bit hypocritical—your staff will already think about the issue instead of devoting truly undivided attention to their personal lives and families. Scheduling the e-mail to be sent at the start of normal working hours takes less than ten seconds in most systems—time worth spent in my view.

If you cannot sleep eight to nine hours a day, at least try to do it before you need to convince others of big projects or upcoming changes. To lead, you must rest as fatigue saps charisma. Researchers asked students to give a speech after waking half of them hourly overnight. Viewers gave sleep-deprived speakers lower marks on charisma. They also rated speakers as less charismatic after their own sleep-deprived night (Barnes et al., 2016).

However, I have noticed a shift in attitude as increasingly sleep is described as the new status symbol (Green, 2017). In the past, everyone was bragging how they worked so many hours that only a few were left for sleeping as a sign of an accomplishment and an unwavering commitment to the organization. Now, stating that you slept well to be ready for the challenges ahead will give you admiration by your staff and your superiors.

A last word about sufficient sleeping as many of you will still note that your commitments and general workload clash with eight to nine hours of daily sleep. Most of us could work 40 hours each day. As we cannot create time, maybe we can learn from highly successful people, such as Charles Darwin and Honoré de Balzac. Darwin slept from midnight to seven in the morning, but then took a nap between 4:00 pm and 5:00 pm in the afternoon; Balzac slept from 6:00 pm in the evening until 1:00 am in the morning, but then napped between 8:00 am and 10:00 am in the morning (Miller, 2014). It looks to me that they listened to their bodies and adjusted their daily routines to what worked for them. I guess they also were not confronted with the relentless commitment to endless meetings that most institutions exhibit today, so their daily routines were less restricting. If you check out the reference, you can compare your routine with the routine of these exceptionally successful people.

Further Readings

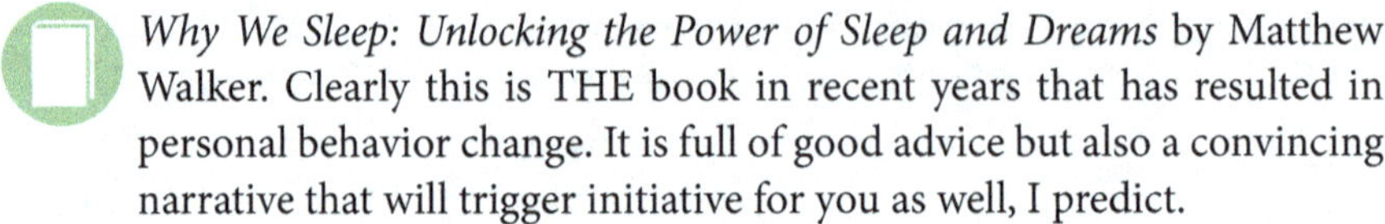

Why We Sleep: Unlocking the Power of Sleep and Dreams by Matthew Walker. Clearly this is THE book in recent years that has resulted in personal behavior change. It is full of good advice but also a convincing narrative that will trigger initiative for you as well, I predict.

Sleep Health Foundation (Sleep Health Foundation, 2020). Australia's leading advocate for healthy sleep provides plenty of resources to improve your sleep. The Website offers educational information designed for the public by sleep experts.

"It is a common experience that a problem difficult at night is resolved in the morning after the committee of sleep has worked on it."
John Steinbeck (1902–1968), American author and the winner of 1962 Nobel Prize in Literature

The Future (of Leadership)

"Now that I have Google+ along with Facebook and Twitter, I won't have to interact with anyone in person ever again."
Andy Borowitz, American writer, comedian, satirist, and actor

What will the future of leadership bring? As technology and our understanding of psychology and genetics develop, how will new findings influence what we should do and how we should conduct ourselves as academic leaders? And, probably most important, who should be selected as a leader for a discipline, a school, a team of professional staff members, a university, or for a city, or a country? And finally, how do we select the leader?

How will diversity influence our leadership debate in the future? What about climate change that causes natural disasters and interrupts supply chains for industries and the stream of international students to Western institutions of higher education? How will the next pandemics influence us and what can we learn from past pandemics (Spielman & Sunavala-Dossabhoy, 2021)? Answers to these questions will have a major influence on how we need to think and lead, now and in the future. I believe that leaders who think deeply about these issues in relation to their institutions will do well and move their organization further.

Should the smartest people lead? The U.S. government under the Kennedy Administration tried that by recruiting Harvard graduates into leading cabinet positions, such as Robert Strange McNamara, a graduate from UC Berkeley and Harvard Business School. These "smart" people played a major role in escalating the United States' involvement in the Vietnam War without any good reason and brought the world to the brink of nuclear war during the Cuban Missile Crisis. On the other hand, **should the most popular person lead?** Thomas Frank claims in his recent book *The People, No: A Brief History of Anti-Populism* that "In political contests in most parts of America, the candidate who captures this refusal of deference is, more often than not, the candidate who wins" (Frank, 2020). Populists, the right-wing nationalist kind, or the left-wing activist kind, are a danger to democracy. According to the U.S. economist Barry Eichengreen, who is also quoted in Frank's book. "Populism arrays the people against the intelligentsia, natives against foreigners, and dominant ethnic, religious, and racial groups against minorities" (Clark, 2020). If political decisions teach us anything about leadership selection, the only conclusion we can draw is that we have not yet figured out how to select the best. The economist Tyler Cowen provides plenty of evidence in his book *Talent* that smart, or high IQ, is overrated when it comes to selecting candidates for leadership positions (Cowen & Gross, 2022).

What about technology? The Internet, Big Data, and information technology in general have dramatically transformed our lives, similarly to the seismic changes that our forebearers experienced during the industrial revolution. Vernor Vinge writes of the future "… we will have the technological means to create superhuman intelligence. Shortly after, the human era will be ended" (Vinge, 1993). Some researchers are afraid of such a dystopian future. Their views are probably best expressed by philosopher Nick Bostrom in his book *Superintelligence* (Bostrom, 2014). Bostrom argues "that accelerating advances in technology will result in drastic changes—social, economic, and, most strikingly, biological—which could converge at a moment of epochal transformation known as the Singularity" (Khatchadourian, 2015).

I am not convinced that a lengthy discussion about AI taking over the affairs of humanity will help us as leaders, but the impact of technology on work life and management is something that contemporary leaders need to be aware of as there are clearly forks in the road ahead. Marshall Brain's novella *Manna* (Brain, 2012) describes two technological views of the future that I find thought-provoking. They are close to my heart as one of them paints the picture of a "super" United States—a dystopian scenario that most Americans will tell you could never happen, but that I, pretending to be the know-it-all global citizen, clearly see as a potential, although undesirable, outcome of trends personally observed over two decades in America. Some of these societal trends, including an individualistic attitude, the concentration of power and wealth, and the reluctance to share beyond the minimal are operationalized in *Manna*, albeit simplistically. The second view is that of a "super" Australia—a communal society that values social justice and places all humans on the same level. After living seven years in Australia, I am still not familiar enough with the Australian psyche, if a coherent one even exists given almost half of all Australians have been born overseas or have parents who have been, to judge if such an outcome would be deemed possible and desirable. Again, the operationalized trends and values seem to match Australia, such as rules driven, happy to share within the rules if they apply to everyone, not worried about people outside our borders and hedonistic. Thus, placing this post-capitalism everyone-contributes-based-on-abilities and everyone-receives-based-on-needs society in Australia was not done by accident. My upbringing in East Germany makes me naturally suspicious of this path—as intriguing as it may sound. I also note that both utopian views posit that privacy is incompatible with an advanced technology-driven society, a view that I share and for which we have plenty of indication, such as the nearly universal lack of inhibition when it comes to sharing private information on social media.

Unleash Creativity Online

As we are struggling to find the best approach to organize work in a hybrid way, we are all trying to find the best mix of how to adapt to this new world where staff expect to be permitted to work at least some days of the week from home. Which tasks can be done best from home, and which tasks require face-to-face interactions? A paper by Melanie Brucks and Jonathan Levav, published in *Nature*, attempts to answer the question of how remote working influences the generation of creative ideas. "Innovation […] relies on collaborative idea generation as the foundation of commercial and scientific progress" (Brucks & Levav, 2022).

Brucks and Levav conducted experiments across different cultures that show that "videoconferencing inhibits the production of creative ideas" due to the differences in the physical nature of videoconferencing and in-person interactions that "focuses communicators on a screen, which prompts a narrower cognitive focus." Their "results suggest that virtual interaction comes with a cognitive cost for creative idea generation." Interestingly, they also found that "when it comes to selecting which idea to pursue, we find no evidence that videoconferencing groups are less effective (and preliminary evidence that they may be more effective) than in-person groups." What does this mean for us who have to navigate our organizations' commitment to providing flexible working options for staff, including staff whose roles require them to be on-site? While our staff might enjoy the benefits of hybrid work, we need to purposefully decide when staff should be directed to be on site. These decisions should not be driven by formulaic approaches to flexible working arrangements but by evidence, such as the results provided by Melanie Brucks and Jonathan Levav.

Can machines outperform leaders? Not yet, but we need to be aware of encroachment into our realm as human decision makers. This is not to support Neo-Luddism, a philosophy that is "based on the concern of the technological impact on individuals, their communities, and/or the environment, Neo-Luddism stipulates the use of the precautionary principle for all new technologies, insisting that technologies be proven safe before adoption, due to the unknown effects that new technologies might inspire" (Wikipedia, 2020b).

In the realm of leadership, data breaches such as seen at Cambridge Analytica (Rosenberg et al., 2018) or Equifax (Newman, 2017) are not the main focus, but rather ethical breaches. For instance, when AI systems make decisions about whether a prospective parolee will re-offend (Angwin & Larson, 2016), or when proprietary software assesses performance of staff and fires them without transparency (Kai-Hsin & Liddicoat, 2018), we quickly learn the importance of the neo-luddite-supported precautionary principle. When will promotion decisions in universities be made by AI? In these and similar cases, AI systems amplify our human prejudices to the detriment of minorities and disadvantaged groups of society. We, as leaders, need to make ethical decisions avoiding blindly relying on technology and we must not blame AI developers for biased decision making. Using AI for reviewing resumes might sound intriguing in comparison to spending another weekend at your desk, but as Amazon managers have learned the hard way, automated resume selection tools unfairly advantaged male applicants because of male dominance in the tech industry (Dastin, 2018). We need to advocate for putting checks and balances in place to avoid going down a slippery slope that eventually takes important decisions out of our hands. Our inherent distrust against computer algorithms making important decisions is best encapsulated in Kahneman's book *Thinking, Fast and Slow* (Kahneman, 2013) when described in a medical context:

> Meehl remarks, "I do not quite know how to alleviate the horror some clinicians seem to experience when they envisage a treatable case being denied treatment because a 'blind, mechanical' equation misclassifies him." In contrast, Meehl and other proponents of algorithms have argued strongly that it is unethical to rely on intuitive judgments for important decisions if an algorithm is available that will make few-

er mistakes. Their rational argument is compelling, but it runs against a stubborn psychological reality: for most people, the cause of a mistake matters. The story of a child dying because an algorithm made a mistake is more poignant than the story of the same tragedy occurring because of human error, and the difference in emotional intensity is readily translated into a moral preference. (p. 229)

Australia, like many other countries, has now developed, supported by its colloquial motto of a "fair go" for all, an ethics framework for AI that proposes as core principles that AI generates net-benefits, does no harm, and follows regulatory and legal compliance, privacy protection, fairness, transparency and explainability, as well as contestability and accountability (Dawson et al., 2019).

I believe that Eric Schmidt, former Google CEO, reflected with a lot of insight on the differences between AI and humans. "We will use human intelligence for judgement, intuition, nuance and uniquely human interactions; we will use computing power for infinite memory, infinitely fast processing and actions limited by human biology. We'll use computers to run predictive correlations from huge volumes of data to track and catch terrorists, but how they are interrogated and handled thereafter will remain the purview of humans and their laws" (Schmidt, 2013).

Should we ban computers from helping us? Absolutely not! What Charles Friedman has framed 15 years ago in the medical context can now easily be applied to the leadership context as well. His fundamental theorem is represented by the equation:

$$(\text{computer} + \text{physician brain}) > \text{physician brain alone}$$

"In words, the theorem stipulates that a person working in partnership with an information resource is 'better' than that same person unassisted. The theorem is applicable to health care, research, education, and administrative activities" (C. P. Friedman, 2009). On a less philosophical note, the COVID-19 pandemic has shown how important information technology can be to maintain business continuity, not only by allowing staff to work remotely, but also by using data to allow distributed decision making facilitating the delegation of decisions that were normally made at the center of the organization. Mike Walsh asked the central question for us as leaders during the pandemic, "What does it take to be an effective leader when there is no one around to lead?" (Walsh, 2020b). He argues in his *Harvard Business Review* article that we need a new "operating system: data is shared transparently, decisions are logged and documented, and there is a high level of data literacy throughout the organization" (Walsh, 2020c). Regardless of pandemic-driven lockdowns, we need to adjust our leadership style to the new reality of managing distributed teams acknowledging that "distributed organizations are driven by small, autonomous teams that are empowered to act with a high degree of independence" (Walsh, 2020c).

Is AI threatening our professional future? Could the advent of this brave new world of AI replace leaders? Managers? As AI tools in all spheres of life are rapidly maturing, they are expected to have a profound impact on many professions including leaders of organizations. There is the general belief that entry-level jobs will be all replaced soon by robots and AI, but that professionals such as lawyers, doctors, accountants, and all kinds of leaders will be spared. This belief results from a confusion between automation and AI. Robots are still dismal when it comes to human tasks such as flipping burgers. Richard Susskind and Daniel Susskind write in *Harvard Business Review*, "expect that within decades the traditional professions will be dismantled, leaving most, but not all, professionals to be replaced by less-expert people, new types of experts, and high-performing systems" (Susskind & Susskind, 2016). The Susskinds define the "AI fallacy" as the view that the only way to get machines to outperform the best human professionals will be to copy the way that these professionals work. They argue that the error here is not recognizing that human professionals are already being outgunned by a combination of brute processing power, big data, and remarkable algorithms. These systems, they correctly point out, do not replicate human reasoning and thinking—they operate differently. So why is the future not all gloom and doom for leaders? My flippant response is that as long as Siri cannot understand my German accent, we are safe. But joking aside, Marcus Tan, CEO and medical director of Health Engine, writes in the healthcare context, and I wholeheartedly believe his statement can be expanded to any other industry: "AI systems are ideally suited to doing the hard, labor intensive work involved in many medical roles, removing the risk of human error and speeding up processes, such as the analysis of huge bulks of data, or raising red flags when something looks risky or concerning. But the human perspective will never be overridden in addressing these red flags. While other industries worry about the impact on jobs, we should always ensure the practitioner is complemented by new tools, never replaced. In short, the machines do the grunt work, and the people apply the nuance" (Tan, 2018).

Leaders cannot remember all information and they cannot remember all the questions to ask. The idea of AI-assisted decision support is to offload memory and raw analysis tasks to the computer, which will then allow leaders to have more time for second-order thinking (Parrish, 2020c) and pondering ethical implications. To paraphrase Zuzana Molčanová "Technology will never replace leaders, but a leader who cannot lead with the help of technology will be replaced by another one who can" (Trevino, 2017).

Context Is Everything

Enrico Coiera reminded us in this Landmark Ideas presentation at Boston's Children Hospital, a Harvard Medical School Teaching Hospital, that "In an age where technology appears to rule supreme, it is easy to forget that our relationship with technology is complicated. Just as humans shape technology, it shapes us in return" (Coiera, 2021). As engineers design software systems that influence how users behave, we as leaders design organizational frameworks and encourage a culture that influences how our people behave. Enrico argues that "Electronic health records for example demand that clinical work bends to the needs of documentation" and I believe that micro-managing staff for example reduces independent judgement and inhibits personal growth. So, when Enrico urges AI researchers in medicine to think of their work not only as "designing algorithms" but as "designing human-machine systems," we need to consider not only sound and sensible delegations, workflows and policies but also how these rules will influence the behavior of our staff in the context of our universities. We need to understand leadership not only as setting up frameworks but using what Enrico calls in his AI world "sociotechnical systems"—a lens that will help us understand unintended consequences.

Here is an example to illustrate what I mean: If we insist that leaders "take full fiscal responsibility of decisions made in their portfolio" by making them approve every $3-paperclip order, we will have to live with the consequences, such as disgruntled leaders as they feel like minions when having to approve hundreds of purchase orders each day, and potentially a lack of scrutiny of high-value purchases as these might get unintentionally approved as part of large batches of low-value orders. When you listen to Enrico's talk, you will be amazed by how many of his examples have implications for our work as academic leaders. For instance, he shared the example of the consequences of data sharing, citing a paper by DesRoches (DesRoches et al., 2020), that showed that clinical notes taken by doctors for personal use are different to notes shared with the team, and again different to notes shared with the patients. So, what about the minutes of meetings? Will minutes be written differently if you share them only with the members of the committee or if you share them with the entire organization? Or, to go a step further, will decisions be made differently if members of a decision-making body know that the widely shared minutes will reflect how they personally decided on important matters? And because of that, will the decisions be more advantageous for the organization due to full transparency, or will decision makers be instead overly cautious because of their perceived sense of heightened scrutiny?

Enrico shares lessons learned from using systems in different contexts, he calls it "transportability." In other words, he talks about the difference between "how work is imagined" versus "work as done." This thought makes me reflect on leadership books and how we need to be very cautious when trying to apply lessons learned elsewhere to our specific organizational context.

How do we prepare for the future? While it is hard to make predictions, we need to keep an open mind when exploring uncharted territory. Wasting energy by resisting change and attempting to keep going as in the past is not helpful. Instead, we should cultivate a mindful optimism and assume that good things will happen if you plan carefully and work hard. I suggest viewing science fiction movies or reading books. With that I do not mean the ones where the aliens invade the earth but am referring to exploratory engineering futuristic works. K. Eric Drexler coined this term that "describe[s] the process of designing and analyzing detailed hypothetical models of systems that are not feasible with current technologies or methods but do seem to be clearly within the bounds of what science considers to be possible within the narrowly defined scope of operation of the hypothetical system model" (Wikipedia, 2020a). Figuring out how these "almost possible" systems, materials, machines, or technologies will influence our current life is a worthwhile exercise that can help us prepare for the not-too-distant future.

We need to explore megatrends and anticipate their impact on us: climate change, massive underemployment, and global pandemics as well as large-scale antimicrobial resistance come to mind. How will these trends affect your university, your school, your team, and your area of inquiry, personally? Exploring the uncertain future is not a reason to become depressed but will help us to cope and be prepared.

Let me conclude with a forecast the inventor Ray Kurzweil made in his 2005 bestseller *The Singularity Is Near* (Kurzweil, 2005): "Those of us who make it to 2045 will live forever, thanks to advances in genetics, nanotechnology (such as nanobots that will course through our bloodstream and repair our bodies from the inside), and artificial intelligence, which will not just figure out how to do all this but recursively improve its own intelligence without limit."

Further Readings

Manna by Marshall Brain (Brain, 2012). This novella is free, not entertaining, about 50 pages long (2-hour read) and touches on many issues at the intersection of technology, artificial intelligence, robotics, well-being, social justice, and ultimately on our responsibility as leaders and members of society.

Superintelligence by Nick Bostrom (Bostrom, 2014). If you want to explore the existential threats to humanity posed by AI, Bostrom's book provides an excellent overview of the topic. Bostrom's central hypothesis is that humans have a poor track record on controlling unintended consequences, for instance, countries have tried to write tax codes without loopholes for centuries and have dismally failed. In extension, AI is like a chess game against the whole world, and we know we are losing against computers.

"Can we build AI without losing control over it?" by Sam Harris (Harris, 2016). Neuroscientist and philosopher Sam Harris explores in his TED talk the existential threats to humanity by AI. Harris says that "[w]e are going to build superhuman machines, but we haven't yet grappled with the problems associated with creating something that may treat us the way we treat ants."

After On: A Novel of Silicon Valley by Rob Reid (Reid, 2017). This novel encapsulates many of the topics discussed in this chapter, including privacy, government intrusion, artificial consciousness, synthetic biology, and much more. Chris Anderson, head of TED, writes about the book "Enter a near-future Silicon Valley that is hilariously, creepily, mind-bogglingly fantastic, yet at the same time all too believable. It might turn out this way. No, really, it might! Along with After On's diabolically ingenious plot, there are crazy-plausible web startups, delicious parodies of social media, and a surprisingly convincing theory of human consciousness."

"Technology Will Replace Many Doctors, Lawyers, and Other Professionals" by Richard Susskind and Daniel Susskind (Susskind & Susskind, 2016). This is a succinct article that explains the AI fallacy very well in my view providing an appreciation for the fact that professionals might be affected by AI faster than they anticipate.

Enlightenment Now: The Case for Reason, Science, Humanism, and Progress by Steven Pinker (Pinker, 2018). I want to end with a last reference that is optimistic and positive. While we all have a tendency to criticize (see Lesson 4: "Build Resilience"), we should look more often at the bright side of life and compare it to how life was only a few decades ago. There is no better book that I know of that can do this better than Pinker's manifesto of optimism: "We are born into a pitiless universe, facing steep odds against life-enabling order and in constant jeopardy of falling apart. We were shaped by a force that is ruthlessly competitive. We are made from crooked timber, vulnerable to illusions, self-centeredness, and at times astounding stupidity. Yet human nature has also been blessed with resources that open a space for a kind of redemption. We are endowed with the power to combine ideas recursively, to have thoughts about our thoughts. We have an instinct for language, allowing us to share the fruits of our experience and ingenuity. We are deepened with the capacity for sympathy—for pity, imagination, compassion, commiseration. These endowments have found ways to magnify their own power." Happy reading!

"We did not come to fear the future. We came here to shape it."
Barack Obama, 44th president of the United States from 2009 to 2017

References

Ackoff, R. L., Addison, H. J., & Bibb, S. (2007). *Management F-Laws: How Organizations Really Work*. Triarchy Press Ltd. https://www.amazon.com/Management-F-Laws-Organizations-Really-Work/dp/0955008123/

Aiken, M. (2016). *The cyber effect: An expert in cyberpsychology explains how technology is shaping our children, our behavior, and our values—and what we can do about it*. Random House. https://www.amazon.com/Cyber-Effect-Cyberpsychology-Technology-Values-ebook/dp/B01A4AXM8M/

Allen, D. (n.d.-a). *Evernote for Mac setup guide*. https://store.gettingthingsdone.com/Evernote-for-Mac-Setup-Guide-p/10430.htm

Allen, D. (n.d.-b). *What is GTD—Getting Things Done*. https://gettingthingsdone.com/what-is-gtd/

Allen, D. (2015). *Getting things done: The art of stress-free productivity* (Revised ed.). Penguin Books. https://www.amazon.com/gp/product/B00KWG9M2E/

Alper, J., & Grossman, C. (2014). *Integrating research and practice: Health system leaders working toward high-value care: workshop summary*. http://www.nap.edu/openbook.php?record_id=18945

Anderson, S. (2009). The benefits of distraction and overstimulation. *New York Magazine*. https://nymag.com/news/features/56793/

Angwin, J., & Larson, J. (2016). *Bias in criminal risk scores is mathematically inevitable, researchers say*. ProPublica. https://www.propublica.org/article/bias-in-criminal-risk-scores-is-mathematically-inevitable-researchers-say

Antonakis, J., Fenley, M., & Liechti, S. (2011). Can charisma be taught? Tests of two interventions. *Academy of Management Learning and Education, 10*(3), 374–396. https://doi.org/10.5465/amle.2010.0012

Argyris, C. (1977). Double loop learning in organizations. *Harvard Business Review*. https://hbr.org/1977/09/double-loop-learning-in-organizations

Argyris, C. (1991). Teaching smart people how to learn. *Harvard Business Review*. 1991-05, Vol.69 (3), p.99-99. https://hbr.org/1991/05/teaching-smart-people-how-to-learn

Asher, R. (1972). *Talking sense*. Pitman.

Ashton, K. (2015). *How to fly a horse*. Cornerstone Digital. https://www.amazon.com.au/gp/product/B00O30HH9U/

Attia, P., & Harris, S. (2018). *#34—Sam Harris, Ph.D.: The transformative power of mindfulness—Peter Attia*. https://peterattiamd.com/samharris/

Australian Institute of Company Directors. (2017). *Board meeting agenda*. https://aicd.companydirectors.com.au/resources/director-tools/practical-tools-for-directors/meeting-effectiveness/board-meeting-agenda

Barach, P. (2000). Reporting and preventing medical mishaps: Lessons from non-medical near miss reporting systems. *BMJ, 320*(7237), 759–763. https://doi.org/10.1136/bmj.320.7237.759

Barnes, C. M., Guarana, C. L., Nauman, S., & Kong, D. T. (2016). Too tired to inspire or be inspired: Sleep deprivation and charismatic leadership. *The Journal of Applied Psychology, 101*(8), 1191–1199. https://doi.org/10.1037/apl0000123

Basu, T. (2015). Here's why email puts you in a nasty mood. *TIME Magazine*, 2015–2016. http://time.com/3985027/email-psychology-work-mood/

Becker, R. (2009). Phänomenologische Forschungen. *JSTOR*, 207–213. http://www.jstor.org/stable/24775233

Bostrom, N. (2014). *Superintelligence: Paths, dangers, strategies*. OUP Oxford. https://www.amazon.com/Superintelligence-Dangers-Strategies-Nick-Bostrom-ebook/dp/B00LOOCGB2/

Boyes, A. (2018). How to focus on what's important, not just what's urgent. *Harvard Business Review*. https://hbr.org/2018/07/how-to-focus-on-whats-important-not-just-whats-urgent

Bradberry, T. (2016). How complaining rewires your brain for negativity. *HuffPost*. https://www.huffpost.com/entry/how-complaining-rewires-y_b_13634470

Brain, M. (2012). *Manna: Two visions of humanity's future*. BYG Publishing.

Brassey, J., Coe, E., Dewhurst, M., Enomoto, K., & Jeffery, B. (2022). Addressing employee burnout: Are you solving the right problem? *McKinsey Health Institute*. https://www.mckinsey.com/MHI/Our-Insights/Addressing-employee-burnout-Are-you-solving-the-right-problem

Brooks, D. (2014). The art of focus. *The New York Times*. https://www.nytimes.com/2014/06/03/opinion/brooks-the-art-of-focus.html

Brooks, D. (2015a). The problem with meaning. *The New York Times*. https://
www.nytimes.com/2015/01/06/opinion/david-brooks-the-problem-with-
meaning.html

Brooks, D. (2015b). *The road to character*. Random House. https://www.
amazon.com/Road-Character-David-Brooks-ebook/dp/B00LYXV61Y/

Brown, B. (2018). *Dare to lead: Brave work. Tough conversations. Whole hearts.*
https://www.amazon.com/Dare-Lead-Brave-Conversations-Hearts-ebook/
dp/B07CWGFPS7

Brucks, M. S., & Levav, J. (2022). Virtual communication curbs creative idea
generation. *Nature, 605*(7908), 108–112. https://doi.org/10.1038/s41586-
022-04643-y

Buchanan, J, Allais, S, Anderson, M, Calvo, R, Peter, S and Pietsch, T (2020)
*The futures of work: what education can and cannot do, Paper prepared for
UNESCO's – Futures of Education Initiative* -[30 pages] https://unesdoc.
unesco.org/ark:/48223/pf0000374435 (and forthcoming in Saar, E and
Robert, P (ed) Handbook of Education and the Labour market, Edward
Elgar)

Burns, H. (2014). 4 "Pearls of wisdom" on how to succeed from a Wall Street
banker. *The Bussiness Journals*. https://www.bizjournals.com/bizjournals/
how-to/growth-strategies/2014/11/carla-harris-morgan-stanley-pearls-of-
wisdom.html

Campuspress. (2020). *About Paul Bloom, Brooks and Suzanne Ragen Professor
of Psychology at Yale University*. https://campuspress.yale.edu/paulbloom/

Carr, N. (2008). Is Google making us stupid? *The Atlantic Monthly, 302*(1),
56–63. https://www.theatlantic.com/magazine/archive/2008/07/is-google-
making-us-stupid/306868/

Carr, N. (2010). *The shallows: What the Internet is doing to our brains*. W. W.
Norton. http://www.amazon.com/The-Shallows-Internet-Doing-Brains/
dp/0393072223

Centola, D. (2021). *Change: How to make big things happen*. John Murray.
https://www.amazon.com.au/gp/product/B0859TZWVG/

Clark, A. (2020). Populism is back in the US election, but not as you know it.
Australian Financial Review. https://www.afr.com/policy/foreign-affairs/
populism-is-back-in-the-us-election-but-not-as-you-know-it-20200817-
p55mfb

Coiera, E. W. (2021). People, Ideas, and Machines. *Landmark Ideas Series*.
https://www.chip.org/events/landmark-ideas-series/people-ideas-and-
machines-video-available

Collins, J. (2005). Level 5 leadership: The triumph of humility and fierce
resolve. *Harvard Business Review*. https://hbr.org/2005/07/level-5-
leadership-the-triumph-of-humility-and-fierce-resolve

Collins, J. (2011). Good to great: Why some companies make the leap...and others don't. *Harper Business*. https://www.amazon.com/Good-Great-Some-Companies-Others-ebook/dp/B0058DRUV6/

Cowen, T., & Gross, D. (2022). *Talent: How to identify energizers, creatives, and winners around the world*. St. Martin's Press. https://www.amazon.com/Talent-Identify-Energizers-Creatives-Winners-ebook/dp/B08R2KNYVX/

Cross, R., Rebele, R., & Grant, A. (2016). Collaborative overload. *Harvard Business Review*. https://hbr.org/2016/01/collaborative-overload

Daley, J. (2021). *Gridlock: Removing barriers to policy reform*. https://grattan.edu.au/report/gridlock/

Dastin, J. (2018). Amazon scraps secret AI recruiting tool that showed bias against women. *Reuters*. https://www.reuters.com/article/us-amazon-com-jobs-automation-insight-idUSKCN1MK08G

Dawson, D., Schleiger, E., Horton, J., McLaughlin, J., Robinson, C., Quezada, G., Scowcroft, J., & Hajkowicz, S. (2019). *Artificial Intelligence: Australia's Ethics Framework*. Data61 CSIRO.

Delistraty, C. C. (2014). To work better, work less. *The Atlantic*. https://www.theatlantic.com/business/archive/2014/08/to-work-better-work-less/375763/

Deresiewicz, W. (2010). Solitude and leadership. *The American Scholar*. https://theamericanscholar.org/solitude-and-leadership/

DesRoches, C. M., Leveille, S., Bell, S. K., Dong, Z. J., Elmore, J. G., Fernandez, L., Harcourt, K., Fitzgerald, P., Payne, T. H., Stametz, R., Delbanco, T., & Walker, J. (2020). The views and experiences of clinicians sharing medical record notes with patients. *JAMA Network Open, 3*(3), e201753. https://doi.org/10.1001/jamanetworkopen.2020.1753

Dominus, S. (2013). Is giving the secret to getting ahead? *The New York Times Magazine*. https://www.nytimes.com/2013/03/31/magazine/is-giving-the-secret-to-getting-ahead.html

Donnelly, T. (2020). Why 5G doesn't cause coronavirus. *Canstar Blue*. https://www.canstarblue.com.au/phone/5g-doesnt-cause-coronavirus/

Dowling, D. (2009). 7 Tips for difficult conversations. *Harvard Business Review*. https://hbr.org/2009/03/7-tips-for-difficult-conversat

Drummond, D. (2012a). *Doctor patient communication: The universal upset patient protocol in healthcare communications*. YouTube. https://www.youtube.com/watch?v=C1YsNGupQhI

Drummond, D. (2012b). Universal Upset Person Protocol Handout. *The Happy MD*. https://www.thehappymd.com/blog/bid/290399/doctor-patient-communication-the-universal-upset-patient-protocol

Dweck, C. (2007). *Mindset: The new psychology of success*. Ballantine Books. http://www.amazon.com/Mindset-The-New-Psychology-Success/dp/0345472322

   A PATH TO ACADEMIC LEADERSHIP

Eggers, D. (2021). *The every: The electrifying follow up to* Sunday Times *bestseller The Circle* (1st ed.). Hamish Hamilton. https://www.amazon.com.au/Every-Dave-Eggers/dp/0241535492/

Ehrlich, O., Fanderl, H., & Habrich, C. (2017). *Mastering the digital advantage in transforming customer experience.* McKinsey & Company. https://www.mckinsey.com/business-functions/operations/our-insights/mastering-the-digital-advantage-in-transforming-customer-experience

Faber, A., & Mazlish, E. (2012). *How to talk so kids will listen & listen so kids will talk.* Scribner. https://www.amazon.com/How-Talk-Kids-Will-Listen-ebook/dp/B005GG0MXI

Ferrazzi, K., & Raz, T. (2014). *Never eat alone, expanded and updated: And other secrets to success, one relationship at a time* (Currency; Exp Upd ed.). https://www.amazon.com/Never-Eat-Alone-Expanded-Updated-ebook/dp/B00H6JBFOS/

Fiorina, C. (2007). *Tough choices: A memoir.* Portfolio. https://www.amazon.com/Tough-Choices-Memoir-Carly-Fiorina/dp/159184181X

Forbes Coaches Council. (2017). 14 Ways to approach conflict and difficult conversations at work. *Forbes.* https://www.forbes.com/sites/forbescoachescouncil/2017/07/17/14-ways-to-approach-conflict-and-difficult-conversations-at-work/?sh=2fec1ec73cfd

Forte, T. (2015a). *Evernote and the brain: Designing creativity workflows.* Evernote Blog. https://evernote.com/blog/designing-creativity-workflows/

Forte, T. (2015b). *One-touch to inbox zero: How I spend 17 minutes per day on email.* Forte Labs Blog. https://fortelabs.co/blog/one-touch-to-inbox-zero/

Forte, T. (2015c). *The secret power of read it later apps.* https://fortelabs.co/blog/the-secret-power-of-read-it-later-apps

Frank, T. (2020). *The people, no: A brief history of anti-populism.* Metropolitan Books. https://www.amazon.com/People-No-Populism-Fight-Democracy/dp/1250220114/

Friedman, C. P. (2009). A "fundamental theorem" of biomedical informatics. *Journal of the American Medical Informatics Association, 16*(1067-5027 (Print)), 169–170.

Friedman, R. (2014). Working too hard makes leading more difficult. *Harvard Business Review.* https://hbr.org/2014/12/working-too-hard-makes-leading-more-difficult

Gawande, A. (2011, October 3). Top athletes and singers have coaches. Should you? *The New Yorker.* http://www.newyorker.com/reporting/2011/10/03/111003fa_fact_gawande

Gazzaley, A., & Rosen, L. D. (2016). *The distracted mind: Ancient brains in a high-tech world.* The MIT Press. https://www.amazon.com/Distracted-Mind-Ancient-Brains-High-Tech-ebook/dp/B08BSYX83P/

Gladwell, M. (n.d.). *Malcolm Gladwell.* https://www.gladwellbooks.com/

Gladwell, M. (2002). *The tipping point: How little things can make a big difference.* Back Bay Books. http://www.amazon.com/The-Tipping-Point-Little-Difference/dp/0316346624

Gladwell, M. (2005). *Blink: The power of thinking without thinking.* Little, Brown. http://www.amazon.com/Blink-The-Power-Thinking-Without/dp/0316172324

Goldsmith, M., & Reiter, M. (2007). *What got you here won't get you there: How successful people become even more successful.* Hachette Books. https://www.amazon.com/What-Got-Here-Wont-There-ebook/dp/B000Q9J128/

Goleman, D. (2000). *Working with emotional intelligence.* Bantam. https://www.amazon.com/Working-Emotional-Intelligence-Daniel-Goleman/dp/0553378589/

Gordon, A. M., & Chen, S. (2014). The role of sleep in interpersonal conflict: Do sleepless nights mean worse fights? *Social Psychological and Personality Science.* https://doi.org/10.1177/1948550613488952

Grabo, A., & van Vugt, M. (2016). Charismatic leadership and the evolution of cooperation. *Evolution and Human Behavior, 37*(5), 399–406. https://doi.org/10.1016/j.evolhumbehav.2016.03.005

Graham, P. (2020). *How to think for yourself.* http://paulgraham.com/think.html

Grant, A. (2013). *Give and take: Why helping others drives our success.* Penguin Books. https://www.amazon.com/Give-Take-Helping-Others-Success-ebook/dp/B00AFPTSI0/

Grant, A. (2020). *Biograhy.* https://www.adamgrant.net/about/biography/

Grant, A. (2021). *Think again: The Power of Knowing What You Don't Know.* Viking.

Green, P. (2017). Sleep is the new status symbol—*The New York Times. The New York Times.* https://www.nytimes.com/2017/04/08/fashion/sleep-tips-and-tools.html

Grice, H. P. (1975). *Logic and conversation.* Harvard University Press. http://courses.media.mit.edu/2004spring/mas966/Grice Logic and Conversation.pdf

Guy, R., & Lownes-Jackson, M. (2010). An examination of students' self-efficacy beliefs and demonstrated computer skills. *Issues in Informing Science & Information Technology Education, 7,* 285–295. https://doi.org/10.28945/1206

Haden, N. K. (2015). *The 9 virtues of exceptional leaders: Unlocking your leadership potential.* Deeds Publishing.

Haidt, J., & Lukianoff, G. (2018). *The coddling of the American mind: How good intentions and bad ideas are setting up a generation for failure.* Penguin

Books. https://www.amazon.com/Coddling-American-Mind-Intentions-Generation-ebook/dp/B076NVFT5P/

Haines, M. (2020). Good governance a steel rod in a crisis. *LinkedIn.* https://www.linkedin.com/pulse/good-governance-steel-rod-crisis-mary-haines/

Halamka, J. (2015a). *Managing up.* Dispatch from the Digital Health Frontier. http://geekdoctor.blogspot.com/2015/07/managing-up.html

Halamka, J. (2015b). *Trajectory not position.* Dispatch from the Digital Health Frontier. http://geekdoctor.blogspot.com/2015/07/trajectory-not-position.html

Hansen, M. T., & Haas, M. R. (2001). Competing for attention in knowledge markets: Electronic document dissemination in a management consulting company. *Administrative Science Quarterly, 46*(1), 1–28.

Harari, Y. N. (2018). *21 Lessons for the 21st century.* Random House. https://www.amazon.com/Lessons-21st-Century-Yuval-Harari-ebook/dp/B079WM7KLS/

Hardin, G. (1968). The tragedy of the commons. *Science, 162*(3859), 1243 LP–1248. https://doi.org/10.1126/science.162.3859.1243

Haribhakti, S. (2020). *Sriram Krishnan, on-demand entertainment critic, social media product leader, and an investor.* SarHaribhakti's Newsletter.

Harris, S. (2014). *Waking up: A guide to spirituality without religion.* Simon & Schuster Export. https://www.amazon.com/Waking-Up-Spirituality-Without-Religion/dp/1476777721

Harris, S. (2016). *Can we build AI without loosing control over it?* TEDSummit. https://www.ted.com/talks/sam_harris_can_we_build_ai_without_losing_control_over_it

Harris, S. (2019). *A Conversation with Adam Grant.* Making Sense. https://www.samharris.org/podcasts/making-sense-episodes/158-understanding-humans-wild

Harris, S. (2020a). *A Conversation with Paul Bloom.* Making Sense Podcast. https://samharris.org/subscriber-extras/188-february-28-2020/

Harris, S. (2020b). *The price of distraction.* Making Sense Podcast. https://samharris.org/subscriber-extras/226-price-distraction/

Harris, S. (2020c). *Waking up Meditation App.* https://wakingup.com/

Harris, S. (2021). A contagion of bad ideas: A conversation with Eric Topol. *Making Sense Podcast.* https://www.samharris.org/podcasts/making-sense-episodes/256-contagion-bad-ideas

Harvard Medical School. (2015). *Harvard Second Generation Study.* Website. https://www.adultdevelopmentstudy.org/

Hastings, N. B., Centore, L. S., Gansky, S. A., Finzen, F. C., White, J. M., Wong, E., Marshall, G. W., Chung, L., & Kalenderian, E. (2018). A novel approach for effective integration of new faculty leadership. *Journal of Healthcare Leadership, 10,* 1–9. https://doi.org/10.2147/JHL.S150493

Haynes, R. B., McKibbon, K. A., Fitzgerald, D., Guyatt, G. H., Walker, C. J., & Sackett, D. L. (1986). How to keep up with the medical literature: VI. How to store and retrieve articles worth keeping. *Annals of Internal Medicine.* https://doi.org/10.7326/0003-4819-105-6-978

Heifetz, R. A. (1994). *Leadership without easy answers.* Harvard University Press. https://www.amazon.com/Leadership-without-Answers-2-Nov-1994-Hardcover/dp/B011T7MS7K/

Heifetz, R. A. (2007). *Perspectives on change: Ronald A. Heifetz.* Change Theorists Wiki. http://changetheorists.pbworks.com/w/page/15475038/RonHeifetz

Heifetz, R. A., & Linsky, M. (2017). *Leadership on the line, with a new preface: Staying alive through the dangers of change.* Harvard Business Review Press. https://www.amazon.com/Leadership-Line-New-Preface-Staying-ebook/dp/B01N1XCO0S/

Heifetz, R., & Linsky, M. (2002). A survival guide for leaders. *Harvard Business Review.* 2002-06, Vol.80 (6), p.65-152. https://hbr.org/2002/06/a-survival-guide-for-leaders

Heller, N. (2020). What if you could outsource your to-do list? *The New Yorker.* https://www.newyorker.com/magazine/2020/12/07/what-if-you-could-outsource-your-to-do-list?utm_source=nl&utm_brand=tny&utm_mailing=TNY_Magazine_113020&utm_campaign=aud-dev&utm_medium=email&bxid=5be9e2302ddf9c72dc4a9acc&cndid=9217500&hasha=5715c67ba6e5714ea

Hess, E. (2017). In the AI age, "being smart" will mean something completely different. *Harvard Business Review.* https://hbr.org/2017/06/in-the-ai-age-being-smart-will-mean-something-completely-different

Hitchens, C. (2007). *God is not great: How religion poisons everything.* Twelve.

Hogan, R. (2007). Personality and the fate of organizations by Robert Hogan. *Personnel Psychology, 60*(4), 1055–1058. https://doi.org/10.1111/j.1744-6570.2007.00101_2.x

Hutson, M. (2016). The charisma effect. *Atlantic.* http://www.theatlantic.com/magazine/archive/2016/09/the-charisma-effect/492740/

Hyatt, M. (2009). *Leadership and the law of replication.* https://michaelhyatt.com/leadership-and-the-law-of-replication/

Institute for Healthcare Improvement. (2020). *Plan-Do-Study-Act (PDSA) worksheet.* https://www.ihi.org/resources/tools/plan-do-study-act-pdsa-worksheet

Iqbal, S. (2022). The rise of the Triple Peak Day. *Microsoft Worklab.* https://www.microsoft.com/en-us/worklab/triple-peak-day

Ireland, T. (2014). What does mindfulness meditation do to your brain? *Scientific American.* https://blogs.scientificamerican.com/guest-blog/what-does-mindfulness-meditation-do-to-your-brain/

Jenkins, R. (2020). Why even good leaders make enemies. *The Chronical of Higher Education.* https://www.chronicle.com/article/why-even-good-leaders-make-enemies

John, D. (2020). Why we all fall foul of the Dunning-Kruger effect. *BBC Reel.* https://www.bbc.com/reel/video/p08d53s8/why-we-all-fall-foul-of-the-dunning-kruger-effect

Jones, D. (1973). Compiled by DuPre Jones. *The New York Times.* https://www.nytimes.com/1973/10/28/archives/the-sayings-of-secretary-henry-language-negotiation-humility-the.html

Junger, S. (2016). *Tribe: On homecoming and belonging.* Twelve.

Kahneman, D. (2013). *Thinking, fast and slow.* Farrar, Straus and Giroux. http://www.amazon.com/Thinking-Fast-Slow-Daniel-Kahneman/dp/0374533555/

Kai-Hsin, H., & Liddicoat, J. (2018). The future of workers' rights in the AI age. *Policy Options.* https://policyoptions.irpp.org/magazines/december-2018/future-workers-rights-ai-age/

Kalberg, S. (1980). Max Weber's types of rationality: Cornerstones for the analysis of rationalization processes in history. *American Journal of Sociology, 85*(5), 1145–1179. https://doi.org/10.1086/227128

Kanowski, S., & Fidler, R. (2021). Meet Ash Barty's mindset coach—Ben Crowe. *Abc Podcast.* https://www.abc.net.au/listen/programs/conversations/ash-barty-sports-mentor-ben-crowe/13418314

Keep, M. (2021a). *Lessons in leadership.* https://youtu.be/k-rzb8UQeZI

Keep, M. (2021b). The silence around miscarriage hurts health care and bereaved parents. *Medical Journal of Australia, 215*(8), 343. https://doi.org/10.5694/mja2.51272

Khatchadourian, R. (2015). The philosopher of Doomsday. *The New Yorker.* https://www.newyorker.com/magazine/2015/11/23/doomsday-invention-artificial-intelligence-nick-bostrom

Khosla, V. (2018). The future of medicine, from a leader in venture capital. *Medscape.* https://www.medscape.com/viewarticle/892034

Killingsworth, M. A., & Gilbert, D. T. (2010). A wandering mind is an unhappy mind. *Science.* https://doi.org/10.1126/science.1192439

Klaasen, D. (2017). Lack of trust is damaging your business—Here's how to fix it. *Blogpost.* https://community.hrdaily.com.au/m/blogpost?id=6416275%3ABlogPost%3A65685

Klein, E. (2021). Obama explain how America went from "Yes we can" to "MAGA." *Ezra Klein Show.* https://www.nytimes.com/2021/06/01/opinion/ezra-klein-podcast-barack-obama.html

Klosterman, C. (2014). My parents paid for my education—Does that mean i need to take a soul-crushing job? *The New York Times Magazine.* https://

www.nytimes.com/2014/08/24/magazine/my-parents-paid-for-my-education-does-that-mean-i-need-to-take-a-soul-crushing-job.html

Kolbert, E. (2017). Why facts don't change our minds. *The New Yorker*. https://www.newyorker.com/magazine/2017/02/27/why-facts-dont-change-our-minds

Kotter, J. P. (2012). *Leading change*. Harvard Business Review Press.

Kruger, J., Epley, N., Parker, J., & Ng, Z.-W. (2005). Egocentrism over e-mail: Can we communicate as well as we think? *Journal of Personality and Social Psychology, 89*(6), 925–936. http://www.ncbi.nlm.nih.gov/pubmed/?term=16393025

Kurzweil, R. (2000). *The age of spiritual machines: When computers exceed human intelligence*. Penguin Books. https://www.amazon.com/Age-Spiritual-Machines-Computers-Intelligence-ebook/dp/B002CIY8JW/

Kurzweil, R. (2005). *The singularity is near: When humans transcend biology*. Penguin Books. https://www.amazon.com/Singularity-Near-Humans-Transcend-Biology-ebook/dp/B000QCSA7C/

Lukianoff, G., & Haidt, J. (2015). The coddling of the American mind. *Atlantic*. https://www.theatlantic.com/magazine/archive/2015/09/the-coddling-of-the-american-mind/399356/

Luo, X., Kanuri, V. K., & Andrews, M. (2013). Long CEO tenure can hurt performance. *Harvard Business Review*. https://hbr.org/2013/03/long-ceo-tenure-can-hurt-performance

Maddock, J. (2020). Your brain's built-in biases insulate your beliefs from contradictory facts. *The Conversation*. https://theconversation.com/your-brains-built-in-biases-insulate-your-beliefs-from-contradictory-facts-150509

Manderscheid, S. V. (2008). New leader assimilation: An intervention for leaders in transition. *Advances in Developing Human Resources, 10*(5), 686–702. https://doi.org/10.1177/1523422308322269

Metzinger, T. (2009). *The ego tunnel: The science of the mind and the myth of the self*. Basic Books.

Mick, D. (2017). 10 Wisdom and mindfulness practices for your personal and professional life. *UVA Today*. https://news.virginia.edu/content/10-wisdom-and-mindfulness-practices-your-personal-and-professional-life

Miller, J. (2014). Infographic: See the daily routines of the world's most famous creative people. *Fast Company*. https://www.fastcompany.com/3028428/infographic-see-the-daily-routines-of-the-worlds-most-famous-creative-people

Mineo, L. (2017). Over nearly 80 years, Harvard study has been showing how to live a healthy and happy life. *Harvard Gazette*. https://news.harvard.edu/gazette/story/2017/04/over-nearly-80-years-harvard-study-has-been-showing-how-to-live-a-healthy-and-happy-life/

Muna, F., & Mansour, N. (2011). Leadership lessons from canada geese. *IEEE Engineering Management Review, 39*(1), 91–99. https://doi.org/10.1109/ EMR.2011.5729977

Murphy, K. (2020). *You're not listening: What you're missing and why it matters.* Celadon Books. https://www.amazon.com/Youre-Not-Listening-Missing- Matters-ebook/dp/B07RYGHKND/

Newman, L. H. (2017). The Equifax breach was entirely preventable. *Wired.* https://www.wired.com/story/equifax-breach-no-excuse/

Newport, C. (2012a). Knowledge workers are bad at working (and here's what to do about it…). *Study Hacks Blog.* https://www.calnewport.com/ blog/2012/11/21/knowledge-workers-are-bad-at-working-and-heres- what-to-do-about-it/

Newport, C. (2012b). *So good they can't ignore you: Why skills trump passion in the quest for work you love.* Grand Central Publishing. https://www. amazon.com/Good-They-Cant-Ignore-You-ebook/dp/B0076DDBJ6/

Newport, C. (2016). *Deep work: rules for focused success in a distracted world.* Piatkus. https://www.amazon.com.au/gp/product/B013UWFM52/

Newport, C. (2019). Was email a mistake? The mathematics of distributed systems suggests that meetings might be better. *The New Yorker.* https:// www.newyorker.com/tech/annals-of-technology/was-e-mail-a-mistake

Nisbett, R. E., & Borgida, E. (1975). Attribution and the psychology of prediction. *Journal of Personality and Social Psychology, 32*(5), 932–943. https://doi.org/10.1037/0022-3514.32.5.932

Norman, D. (1991). Cognitive artifacts. In J. M. Carroll (Ed.), *Designing interaction: Psychology at the human-computer interface* (pp. 17–38). Cambridge University Press.

O'Donnell, J. A., Modesto, A., Oakley, M., Polk, D. E., Valappil, B., & Spallek, H. (2013). Sealants and dental caries: Insight into dentists' behaviors regarding implementation of clinical practice recommendations. *Journal of the American Dental Association, 144*(4), e24–30. http://jada.ada.org/ content/144/4/e24.long

Obama, B. (2020). *How I approach the toughest decisions.* Medium. https:// barackobama.medium.com/how-i-approach-the-toughest-decisions- dc1b165cdf2d

Oblinger, D. (2008). Growing up with Google: What it means to education. *Emerging Technologies for Learning, 3,* 11–28.

Osheroff, J. A. (2009). *Improving medication use and outcomes with clinical decision support: A step-by-step guide.* Healthcare Information and Management Systems Society.

Packer, G. (2014). The astonishing rise of Angela Merkel—*The New Yorker.* *The New Yorker.* https://www.newyorker.com/?p=2903737&mbid=social_ tablet_e

Parrish, S. (2019). Mental models: The best way to make intelligent decisions (109 models explained). *Farnam Street*. https://fs.blog/mental-models/

Parrish, S. (2020a). Hanlon's razor: Relax, not everything is out to get you. *Farnam Street*. https://fs.blog/2017/04/mental-model-hanlons-razor/

Parrish, S. (2020b). Resonance: How to open doors for other people. *Farnam Street*. https://fs.blog/2019/05/resonance-open-doors/

Parrish, S. (2020c). Second-order thinking: What smart people use to outperform. *Farnam Street*. https://fs.blog/2016/04/second-order-thinking/

Parrish, S. (2020d). The Buffett formula: Going to bed smarter than when you woke up. *Farnam Street*. https://fs.blog/2013/05/the-buffett-formula/

Parrish, S. (2020e). Why we focus on trivial things: The Bikeshed effect. *Farnam Street*. https://fs.blog/2020/04/bikeshed-effect/

Parrish, S. (2021). *Matt Ridley: Infinite Innovation*. Farnam Street (FS). https://fs.blog/knowledge-project-podcast/matt-ridley/

Parrish, S. (2022a). Positive asymmetry. *Farnam Street* (Newsletter, No. 462). https://fs.blog/brain-food/march-6-2022/

Parrish, S. (2022b). Sarah Jones Simmer: The foundation of trust. *The Knowledge Project*. https://fs.blog/knowledge-project-podcast-transcripts/sarah-jones-simmer/

Parrish, S. (2022c). Thomas Zurbuchen: Adventures in astrophysics. *Farnam Street Media Inc., The Knowledge Project*. https://fs.blog/knowledge-project-podcast/thomas-zurbuchen/

Parrish, S. (2022d). Why you should practice failure. *Farnam Street*.

Perlmutter, D. D. (2019a). Admin 101. *The Chronical of Higher Education*. https://www.chronicle.com/package/admin-101/

Perlmutter, D. D. (2019b). How to manage the strategic-planning process. *The Chronicle*. https://www.chronicle.com/article/admin-101-how-to-manage-the-strategic-planning-process/

Pinker, S. (2011). *The Better Angels of Our Nature: Why Violence Has Declined*. Viking. https://www.amazon.com/Better-Angels-Our-Nature-Violence/dp/0670022950/

Pinker, S. (2018). *Enlightenment now: The case for reason, science, humanism, and progress*. Penguin Books. https://www.amazon.com/Enlightenment-Now-Science-Humanism-Progress-ebook/dp/B073TJBYTB/

Pinker, S. (2021). *Rationality: What it is, why it seems scarce, why it matters*. Viking. https://www.amazon.com/Rationality-What-Seems-Scarce-Matters-ebook/dp/B08WK3JNLT/

Piper, K. (2021). How does progress happen? *Vox*. https://www.vox.com/future-perfect/22652782/roots-of-progress-jason-crawford

Pipes, T. (2016). Taking note: What commonplace books can teach us about our past. *Evernote Blog*. https://evernote.com/blog/taking-note-commonplace-books/

Pisano, G. P. (2019). The hard truth about innovative cultures. *Harvard Business Review*. https://hbr.org/2019/01/the-hard-truth-about-innovative-cultures

Plomin, R. (2018). *Blueprint: How DNA makes us who we are*. The MIT Press.

Plummer, M., & Wilson, J. (2018). The lie that perfectionists tell themselves. *Harvard Business Review*. https://hbr.org/2018/05/the-lie-that-perfectionists-tell-themselves

Porath, C. (2015). No time to be nice at work. *The New York Times*. https://www.nytimes.com/2015/06/21/opinion/sunday/is-your-boss-mean.html

Porath, C. (2018). *Why being respectful to your coworkers is good for business, TED Talk*. https://www.ted.com/talks/christine_porath_why_being_respectful_to_your_coworkers_is_good_for_business

Prelinger, M. (2011). Yuri's Day from an anti-nostalgia perspective. *The Atlantic*. https://www.theatlantic.com/technology/archive/2011/04/yuris-day-from-an-anti-nostalgia-perspective/237150/

Raid, E. (2015). Why some men pretend to work 80-hour weeks. *Harvard Business Review*. https://hbr.org/2015/04/why-some-men-pretend-to-work-80-hour-weeks

Reddit. (2020). *The front page of the Internet*. https://www.reddit.com/

Reid, R. (2017). *After on: A novel of silicon valley*. Del Rey. https://www.amazon.com/After-Silicon-Valley-Rob-Reid-ebook/dp/B06XZSNB3W/

Renahan, M. (2018). *The ideal length of a sales email, based on 40 million emails*. HubSpot. https://blog.hubspot.com/sales/ideal-length-sales-email

Ricard, M., & Singer, W. (2017). Neuroscience has a lot to learn from Buddhism. *The Atlantic*. https://www.theatlantic.com/international/archive/2017/12/buddhism-and-neuroscience/548120/

Rosenberg, M., Confessore, N., & Cadwalladr, C. (2018). How Trump consultants exploited the Facebook data of millions. *The New York Times*. https://www.nytimes.com/2018/03/17/us/politics/cambridge-analytica-trump-campaign.html

Ruscio, K. P. (2020). Leaders like Trump fail if they cannot speak the truth and earn trust. *The Conversation*. https://theconversation.com/leaders-like-trump-fail-if-they-cannot-speak-the-truth-and-earn-trust-141767

Russ, J. (2008). Interview with Clay Shirky, Part I. *Columbia Journalism Review*. https://archives.cjr.org/overload/interview_with_clay_shirky_par.php?page=all

Save emails into Evernote. (2020). Evernote Blog. https://help.evernote.com/hc/en-us/articles/209005347

Schmidt, E. (2013). Google chairman Eric Schmidt says leaders still matter. *The Business Journals*. https://www.upstart.bizjournals.com/entrepreneurs/hot-shots/2013/05/07/eric-schmidt-says-leaders-still-matter.html

Schwartz, T., & Porath, C. (2014). Why you hate work. *The New York Times*. https://www.nytimes.com/2014/06/01/opinion/sunday/why-you-hate-work.html

Shenk, J. W. (2009). What makes us happy? *The Atlantic*. https://www.theatlantic.com/magazine/archive/2009/06/what-makes-us-happy/307439/

Simon, H. A. (1957). *Models of man, social and rational: Mathematical essays on rational human behaviour in a social setting*. Wiley.

Simpson, S., & Du Plessis, S. (2015). *A culture turned: Using UGRs to boost performance and culture*. CreateSpace Independent Publishing Platform. https://www.amazon.com/Culture-Turned-Using-performance-culture/dp/1481017659

Sleep Health Foundation. (2020). https://www.sleephealthfoundation.org.au/

Slim, W. (1957). Leadership in management. *Australian Army Journal*, 5–13. http://intergon.net/slim.html

Sokol, D. (2012). How to be a cool headed clinician. In *BMJ (Online)*. https://doi.org/10.1136/bmj.e3980

Spallek, H. (2024). *Leadership Travel Guide Newsletter*. https://www.spallek.com/leadership

Spielman, A. I., & Sunavala-Dossabhoy, G. (2021). Pandemics and education: A historical review. *Journal of Dental Education, 85*(6), 741–746. https://doi.org/10.1002/jdd.12615

Stamoulis, D. T. (2015). *Senior executive assessment: A key to responsible corporate governance*. Wiley-Blackwell. https://www.amazon.com/Senior-Executive-Assessment-Responsible-Governance-ebook/dp/B017OG3CFM/

Stamoulis, D. T. (2017). *Results intelligence: Identifying people who get things done*. https://www.russellreynolds.com/insights/thought-leadership/results-intelligence-identifying-people-who-get-things-done#

Stone, D., Patton, B., & Heen, S. (2010). *Difficult conversations: How to discuss what matters most*. Penguin Books. https://www.amazon.com/Difficult-Conversations-Discuss-What-Matters/dp/0143118447/

Susskind, R., & Susskind, D. (2016). Technology will replace many doctors, lawyers, and other professionals. *Harvard Business Review*. https://hbr.org/2016/10/robots-will-replace-doctors-lawyers-and-other-professionals

Talbot, M. (2021). Is it really too late to learn new skills? *The New Yorker*. https://www.newyorker.com/magazine/2021/01/18/is-it-really-too-late-to-learn-new-skills

Tan, M. (2018). *Overcoming fear, removing barriers and embracing the limitless potential of AI in healthcare*. Healthcare IT News Australia. https://www.healthcareit.com.au/opinion/overcoming-fear-removing-barriers-and-embracing-limitless-potential-ai-healthcare

Tapia, A., Polonskaia, A., Wang, Y.-A., Hezlett, S., & Orr, E. (2020). Head and heart: Inclusive leaders for an equitable future. *Korn-Ferry*.

The Resilience Institute. (2020). https://resiliencei.com/

Thompson, D. (2017). Google X and the science of radical creativity. *Atlantic*. https://www.theatlantic.com/magazine/archive/2017/11/x-google-moonshot-factory/540648/

Thompson, D. (2022). This is what happens when there are too many meetings: Why a 9-to-10 is the new 9-to-5. *The Atlantic*. https://www.theatlantic.com/newsletters/archive/2022/04/triple-peak-day-work-from-home/629457/

Thoreau, H. D. (1854). *Walden: or, Life in the woods*. https://www.goodreads.com/work/quotes/2361393-walden-or-life-in-the-woods

Tingle, L. (2018). Follow the leader: Democracy and the rise of the strongman. *Quarterly Essay, 71*, 1–90.

Tolle, E. (2010). *The power of now: A guide to spiritual enlightenment*. New World Library.

Treasure, J. (2013). How to speak so that people want to listen. *TED Global 2013*. https://www.ted.com/talks/julian_treasure_how_to_speak_so_that_people_want_to_listen

Trevino, D. (2017). *Technology will never replace teachers*. Microsoft Education Blog. https://educationblog.microsoft.com/en-us/2017/11/technology-will-never-replace-teachers-but-a-teacher-who-cannot-teach-with-technology-will-be-replaced-by-another-one-who-can-zuzana-molcanova-slovakia/

Updike, J. (2009). *More matter: Essays and criticism*. Random House. https://www.amazon.com/More-Matter-Criticism-John-Updike-ebook/dp/B0030CMK7Q/

Useem, J. (2017). Power causes brain damage. *The Atlantic*. https://www.theatlantic.com/magazine/archive/2017/07/power-causes-brain-damage/528711/

Van Der Helm, E., Gujar, N., & Walker, M. P. (2010). Sleep deprivation impairs the accurate recognition of human emotions. *Sleep*. https://doi.org/10.1093/sleep/33.3.335

van Knippenberg, D., Dahlander, L., Haas, M. R., & George, G. (2015). Information, attention, and decision making. *Academy of Management Journal, 58*(3), 649–657. https://doi.org/10.5465/amj.2015.4003

Veldhoen Company. (2022). *Rethink the way we work*. https://www.veldhoencompany.com/en/activity-based-working/

Vinge, V. (1993). Vernor Vinge on the singularity. *Whole Earth Review*. https://mindstalk.net/vinge/vinge-sing.html

Vinge, V. (2007). Rainbows end. *Tor Science Fiction*. http://www.amazon.com/Rainbows-End-Vernor-Vinge/dp/0812536363

von Hippel, W., Ronay, R., Baker, E., Kjelsaas, K., & Murphy, S. C. (2016). Quick thinkers are smooth talkers: Mental speed facilitates charisma. *Psychological Science, 27*(1), 119–122. https://doi. org/10.1177/0956797615616255

von Rueden, C. (2020). Nature and nurture both contribute to gender inequality in leadership—but that doesn't mean patriarchy is forever. *The Conversation.* https://theconversation.com/nature-and-nurture-both-contribute-to-gender-inequality-in-leadership-but-that-doesnt-mean-patriarchy-is-forever-123311

Waldinger, R. (2015). What makes a good life? Lessons from the longest study on happiness. *TED Talk.* https://www.ted.com/talks/robert_waldinger_what_makes_a_good_life_lessons_from_the_longest_study_on_happiness/transcript?language=en

Walker, M. (2017). Why we sleep: Unlocking the power of sleep and dream (Illustrate). *Scribner.* https://www.amazon.com/Why-We-Sleep-Unlocking-Dreams-ebook/dp/B06ZZ1YGJ5

Walsh, M. (2020a). *Remote work doesn't work, if you don't rethink meetings.* https://www.mike-walsh.com/blog/remote-work-doesnt-work-if-you-dont-rethink-meetings

Walsh, M. (2020b). *The best way to lead is to be led by data.* Mike Walsh Blog. https://www.mike-walsh.com/blog/the-best-way-to-lead

Walsh, M. (2020c). The key to building a successful remote organization? Data. *Harvard Business Review.* https://hbr.org/2020/05/the-key-to-building-a-successful-remote-organization-data

Watson, J., & Wilson, E. O. (2009). An intellectual Entente. *Harvard Magazine.* https://harvardmagazine.com/breaking-news/james-watson-edward-o-wilson-intellectual-entente

Web clipper: Save web pages, articles, and PDFs. (2021). Evernote Blog. https://evernote.com/features/webclipper

Wikipedia. (2020a). Exploratory engineering. https://en.wikipedia.org/wiki/Exploratory_engineering

Wikipedia. (2020b). Neo-Luddism. https://en.wikipedia.org/wiki/Neo-Luddism#cite_note-christensenencyclopedia-4

Williams, J. M. (2013). *Style: Lessons in clarity and grace* (11th ed.). Pearson. https://www.amazon.com/Style-Lessons-Joseph-M-Williams-ebook/dp/B00BFFGGGG/

Young, S. (2017). 6 Techniques to nurture an agile mind. *LinkedIn.* https://www.linkedin.com/pulse/6-techniques-nurture-agile-mind-sarah-young/

Zak, P. J. (2017). *Trust factor: The science of creating high-performance companies.* AMACOM. https://www.amazon.com/Trust-Factor-Creating-High-Performance-Companies-ebook/dp/B01HUER0ZG/

Zeng, X., Chiu, C. P. K., Wang, R., Oei, T. P. S., & Leung, F. Y. K. (2015). The effect of loving-kindness meditation on positive emotions: A meta-analytic review. *Frontiers in Psychology*, 6(NOV), 1693. https://doi.org/10.3389/fpsyg.2015.01693

Zhu, M., Yang, Y., & Hsee, C. K. (2018). The mere urgency effect. *Journal of Consumer Research*, 45(3), 673–690. https://doi.org/10.1093/jcr/ucy008

www.ingramcontent.com/pod-product-compliance
Lightning Source LLC
Chambersburg PA
CBHW071249150726

48001CB00018B/476